Cookin' in the Keys

Memories of Sights and Tastes In the Florida Keys

by
WILLIAM FLAGG

Second Edition

Published by
Palm Island Press
411 Truman Avenue, Key West, Florida 33040 U.S.A.
pipress@earthlink.net   SAN 298-4024

Library of Congress Cataloging in Publication Data

Flagg, William G., 1934-
Cookin' in the Keys.

1. Cookery—Florida—Florida Keys. I. Title.
TX715.F576 1985   641.5   84-27176
ISBN 0-9643434-0-6

Manufactured in the United States of America

*Sincere thanks to cover artist, Elizabeth E. Mitchell. For more
fabulous tropical art visit her website at www.resilk.com*

Preface

Agnes and I first came to the Keys, and to Key West, for a winter vacation in January of 1980. Although I did a bit of writing that winter, the time was mostly spent enjoying the sun, learning how to fish and crab, seeing the sights and trying out the local restaurants.

After two pleasant months we left, looking forward to other adventures in other places, never thinking that we'd return. Wrong! Back we came in the fall of 1981 to again spend the winter, this time for almost six months. Again we left for the summer, but this time we were saying "See you in the fall" rather than "Goodbye".

Sure enough, in the fall we did return...loaded down with clothes, most of my cookbook reference library and a ton of pots, pans and other kitchen gadgets. This time we built a house and now we call Key West, in the Conch Republic... home!

Naturally it wasn't long before I was seeking out and testing local recipes, developing friendships with food oriented folks like myself and discovering which of the many fine restaurants could entice me to return.

I quickly discovered that the foods of Key West were influenced by a variety of considerations...

Cuba's only 90 miles away and the many Cubans who migrated here brought with them their favorite dishes.

The bountiful sea which surrounds us, providing us with a rich harvest of fish, conch, crab, lobster and shrimp.

Key West is a "Navy" town and the Navy wives bring recipes collected from all over the world. Snowbirds (people who fly North for the summer and then migrate back in the fall) also abound, bringing recipes from all over the United States and Canada.

Key West is in the tropics...and fruits such as
Key lime, banana, mango, papaya, coconut...to mention just
a few, abound. Naturally, these delicious foods influence the
recipes which are popular here.

Topping it all off, Key West is a true resort city, with
excellent restaurants of all types, each competing with its
culinary skill for the tourist dollar.

Is it any wonder that I faithfully walk four miles a day...
and still continually find myself dieting?

At any rate, researching recipes here in the Keys is as much
fun as I know...and I hope this little book allows you to
go back to wherever you call home, with many pleasant
memories of your visit, as well as the ability to recreate
some of the dishes you enjoyed while you were in the Keys.

WILLIAM G. FLAGG

Credits

Thanks are due to old friends and new...To old friends
who came to visit, asking questions about Florida Keys
cooking and who became the cast of characters in this book.

Thanks also to the many new friends; Conchs and would-be
Conchs, for sharing treasured recipes and folklore with this
researcher. In those instances where recipes were offered
by others, acknowledgement is given below the recipe.

Toni Murray did the typing, as well as suggesting many
improvements. The sketches of local scenes were done by
Cory Wild.

Without their encouragement, suggestions and help, this book
would never have been created.

Guide to Contents

Illustrations

The Cuban Influence

Key West is only 90 miles from Cuba. (Miami is 156 miles away.)
For many years...and in many ways...Key West was more "Cuban"
than "U.S.". In 1912 Henry Flagler physically joined Key West to the
United States when he built his famous railroad. But even that
railroad tied this island closer to Cuba...because that train brought
many vacationers to Key West and they immediately boarded ferries
to go to Cuba.

Today, there is a large permanent Cuban population in the city.
Spanish is an often heard second language; and during your visit to
Key West, you really must try one of the many excellent Cuban
restaurants.

The following recipes offer a sampling of some of the fine Cuban
dishes you'll find.

Cuban Pork Roast Dinner

It's not only country music stars that travel around the country in converted buses. About twenty years ago, imaginative campers began converting old buses to luxurious motor homes. This was primarily because

(a)   There were no companies making motor homes.
(b)   Used buses were cheap.

Anyway, one of my best friends (almost an older brother), named John Case, recently converted a used bus into a truly beautiful home on wheels.

His "shakedown" cruise brought him from his home in Massachusetts down to my new home in Key West. With him on this trip came friends in two other buses, traveling in caravan for 2,000 miles ... and then only two people step out of each!

In honor of their arrival, I decided to invite them (and a gang of other nice people) to a Cuban meal. Here's the menu for this typical Key West meal.

Cuban Roast Pork
topped with Raw Onion Rings
Black Beans • Yellow Rice
Fried Plantain • Yuca
Hot Buttered Cuban Bread
Sangria
Cafe Con Leche • Leche Flan

To serve, first a liberal portion of roast pork is placed on each plate, topped with several onion rings. Also on the plate is arranged a scoop of yellow rice and a few pieces each of plantain and yuca. A scoop full of black beans is placed on a side dish.

Some folks eat the beans and rice as two separate dishes, but those in the know will make a depression in their rice and fill this "well" with two or three generous spoonfuls of beans. As they eat the mixture of beans and rice, the beans are replenished from the cup.

As most of the food is fairly dry, guests will be thirsty. So, place
at least one pitcher of Sangria on the table, preferably more.

Now…you're ready to enjoy the feast.

Once your guests have finished the meal and are leaning
back in their chairs rubbing their too-full bellies, show them
no mercy!

Bring out the Cafe Con Leche and Leche Flan. The coffee will
set the meal just perfectly and everyone will find room
for just a "small" piece of the flan.

This recipe calls for one clove of garlic per pound
of fresh pork. To prepare the meat for marinating, I
use a small funnel and a chop stick. Whatever method
you choose to accomplish the job, your guests will rave
over the tender, delicious and spicy-sweet result. This
recipe is for 40 people, but can be adjusted down for
any size group.

Cuban Roast Pork

INGREDIENTS (serves 40)

1		Fresh leg of pork (about 20 pounds)
20	Cloves	Garlic, diced
3	Tbsps.	Oregano
1	Cup	Key lime juice
1	Tbsp.	Salt
1	Tsp.	Black pepper, freshly ground

DIRECTIONS

- With a sharp boning knife, make deep incisions at 2 inch intervals all over the pork.

- Combine the garlic and oregano.

- Place the funnel over one of the knife holes in the pork. Place about one teaspoon of the garlic-oregano mixture into the funnel.

- With a chop stick, push the mixture down through the mouth of the funnel and deep into the pork.

* Repeat this process with the remaining holes, until the entire pork is impregnated with the mixture.

* Pour lime juice all over the pork and then sprinkle it with salt and pepper. Allow to marinate overnight in the refrigerator.

* Pour off the marinade and place the pork onto a rack, skin side down, in a roasting pan.

* Roast, in a preheated 350° oven, for one hour.

* Carefully turn roast, so that skin side is up. Turn temperature down to 275°. Insert a meat thermometer into the center of the roast, making certain that the inner tip is in meat and not near bone. Continue roasting until inner temperature is 185°. Total cooking time will be about 30 minutes per pound.

* Allow to "rest" for about 20 minutes before carving.

Whole Roasted Pig, Coffin Style

I'm a member the Key West chapter of the United States Power Squadron, an organization which has been established to actively promote safe boating practices. When the members are not busy teaching safe boating, they have been known to throw some really great parties. Each year one of the best is their Cuban Pig Roast… where each guest supplements the roast with a potluck dish (vegetable or dessert).

Naturally the dishes brought by the guests are fabulous…but the way the pork is cooked is just extraordinary.

Because special equipment is used, you probably can't duplicate the roast. However, as the cooking method was unique, I thought you might like to hear about it.

- A whole pig is used. After it has been cleaned, etc., it is split almost through from front to back…and then spread and secured between two large racks. The racks have two handles on each side for use in lifting and turning the pig.

- The rack is centered in a large coffin-shaped metal container (about 2 1/2' wide by 6' long by 1' high) which has about an inch of water in the bottom.

- A cover is placed on top and a charcoal fire is built on the cover. The charcoal is spread evenly over the cover and the pig, located centrally inside the container, is slowly roasted. Periodically the roasting pig is turned so that the skin becomes a crispy golden brown.

- Apparently, the water in the bottom keeps the internal temperature below 212°, resulting in pork that literally melts in your mouth.

Black Beans and Rice

INGREDIENTS (serves 6 to 8)

1	Pound	Dried black beans, washed and drained
6	Cups	Water
1/2	Cup	Olive oil
1	Large	Onion, coarsely chopped
		Green bell pepper, stem and seeds removed, coarsely chopped
1	Clove	Garlic minced
2		Bay leaves
2	Tsps.	Salt
1/4	Tsp.	Black pepper, freshly ground
1		Smoked ham bone (optional)
1	Slice	Bacon, minced
1/4	Cup	Wine vinegar
		Cooked yellow rice
		Raw rings of onion or scallions cut into 1/4 inch rounds

DIRECTIONS

• Cover beans with water. Bring to a boil and boil for two minutes. Remove from heat, cover pan and let stand for one hour.

• Heat olive oil in skillet. Add onion, pepper and garlic. Saute for about 5 minutes. Add to beans.

• Add the bay leaves, salt, pepper, ham bone and bacon. Bring to a boil and simmer, covered, for two hours, adding more water if necessary, until tender.

• Remove bay leaves and add the wine vinegar. Serve with yellow rice, garnished with onion rings.

NOTES

• This dish can be improved through the use of any flavorful stock, rather than water. Use chicken or ham stock, vegetable cooking water, a little dry white wine, etc.

BLACK BEANS AND RICE (continued)

- As the dish simmers, consider adding:

    - 1/2 cup of pimiento stuffed olives, sliced
    - 1 teaspoon ground oregano
    - 1/4 teaspoon ground cumin

- Do not add vinegar until end of cooking time because the acid slows down the softening process.

- Cooked beans freeze well.

- To cook yellow rice, just cook rice as you normally do, but add a drop or two of yellow food color. In Key West, most cooks use an inexpensive condiment called BIJOL, which gives rice a rich yellow color.

Plantain

Many Cuban-style meals in Key West are served with slices of sauteed plantain, a starchy, banana-shaped fruit, which tastes somewhat like yams.

To select plantains: Choose ripe black-skinned plantains.
Plan on 3 to 4 servings from each plantain.

To prepare for cooking: Peel, just as you would a banana.
Cut into 1/4 inch slices, on the bias, so slices are oval.

To sauté: Sauté in 1/4 cup butter, over moderate heat, turning often, for 15 to 20 minutes, until tender.

To serve: Plan on 3 or 4 slices per person.

Here's another recipe, slightly sweeter than regular plantain, that you might enjoy.

Candied Plantain

INGREDIENTS (serves 6-8)

4	Ripe	Plantains (skin will be black) , peeled and sliced
1	Tbsp.	Salad oil
2	Tsps.	Brown sugar
3/4	Tsp.	Cinnamon
1/4	Tsp.	Nutmeg

DIRECTIONS

- Place sliced plantain in skillet with oil. Sprinkle brown sugar, cinnamon and nutmeg.

- Fry on low heat until browned and then turn over and fry until cooked through and browned.

NOTE:

- More oil may be required during cooking.

Modish James
Key West Citizen
Cooking Contest

Yuca is served as one of several side dishes for many Cuban meals. It is the Cuban (or Spanish) word for casava. When cooked, this starchy root tastes very much like roasted chestnuts.

Yuca Cocida (French Fried Cassava)

INGREDIENTS (serves 8, as a vegetable dish)

4	Cups	Water
1	Package	Frozen yuca (28 ounces)
1	Tsp.	Salt
1/8	Tsp.	White pepper
2	Tbsps.	Lemon juice
2	Tbsps.	Vegetable oil
1	Tbsp.	Parmesan cheese

DIRECTIONS

- Pour water into a 4 quart saucepan. Heat to a boil. Add frozen yuca to water. Cover and boil for 30 minutes, or until tender. Drain.

- Cut into one inch pieces. Sprinkle with salt, pepper and lemon juice.

- Heat oil in a large skillet and fry the yuca until crisp and lightly browned. Sprinkle with Parmesan cheese. Serve hot.

As mentioned earlier, Key West is but 90 miles from Cuba. (It's 154 miles to Miami.) When Henry Flagler built his famous railroad to Key West, it was to bring customers to the ferry, which then took them for a visit to Cuba. One of the more beautiful buildings in Key West is the former Cuban Ambassador's residence and there are parts of this town where English is the second language, if it's spoken at all. Naturally there are several Cuban bakeries and one of the more popular products is Cuban bread…similar in shape to French bread, but lighter and crisper. When served in restaurants, it's cut in half lengthwise, liberally buttered and then reheated…to be served hot and crispy, almost dripping with butter.

Cuban Bread

INGREDIENTS (makes 2 loaves)

1	Package	Dry yeast (or 1 cake of yeast)
2	Cups	Water, lukewarm
1 1/4	Tsps.	Salt
1	Tbsp.	Sugar
6 to 9	Cups	All purpose flour

DIRECTIONS

- Dissolve the yeast in the warm water. Add the salt and sugar and mix thoroughly.

- Add the flour, a cup at a time, while mixing it with a dough hook on an electric mixer at low speed. Add enough flour to make a smooth dough. Mix thoroughly. The amount of flour will depend upon its ability to absorb moisture.

- Cover it with a clean towel and put it in a warm spot (80° to 90°), where there are no drafts.

- Observe its initial size and then let it rise until the dough is double in volume, about 1 1/2 to 2 hours. Deflate the dough by punching it 2 or 3 times.

CUBAN BREAD (continued)

- Turn the dough out onto a lightly floured board and divide into two balls. Shape by stretching and rolling each piece of dough into a long sausage shape about 1 1/2 inches in diameter.

- Arrange the loaves well apart on an ungreased baking sheet which has been heavily sprinkled with cornmeal. Allow to rise for 5 minutes.

- Slash the tops of the loaves in three or four places, brush them with water, and place them in a cold oven.

- Turn the oven on and set it for 400°. Add a pan of boiling water to the oven and bake the loaves until crusty and done, about 40 to 45 minutes. When done, they will sound rather hollow when tapped lightly on top.

This is a very popular dish with the many families of Cuban background who live in Key West.

Picadillo

INGREDIENTS (serves 20)

1/4	Cup	Cooking oil
5	Cups	Onion, coarsely chopped
10	Cloves	Garlic, minced
5	Pounds	Lean ground beef
1 1/2	Cups	Dry white wine
1	Can	Whole, peeled tomatoes (28 ounces)
1	Can	Tomato sauce (15 ounces)
1	Can	Tomato paste (6 ounces)
4	Tsps.	Salt
1 1/2	Tsps.	Black pepper, freshly ground
2	Tsps.	Monosodium glutamate (optional)
2	Tsps.	Oregano
3/4	Tsp.	Cinnamon
1/4	Tsp.	Ground Cloves
2	Cups	Dark or light raisins, plumped up in hot water
1 1/2	Cups	Pimiento-stuffed olives, sliced in thirds
3		Green bell peppers, stem and seeds removed, diced
2		Jalapeno peppers, stem and seeds removed, finely diced
1	Cup	Blanched almonds

DIRECTIONS

- Heat oil in a large Dutch oven. Add onion and garlic. Saute for about 15 minutes, until golden. Add the ground beef and saute for 20 minutes, breaking up any clumps.

- Blend in the wine, the tomatoes, tomato sauce, tomato paste, salt, pepper, MSG, oregano, cinnamon and cloves. Allow to simmer gently, uncovered, for 45 minutes to blend flavors.

PICADILLO (continued)

- Stir in the raisins, olives, bell and Jalapeno peppers, and the almonds. Reheat and allow to simmer for about 5 minutes.

- Serve over or with hot fluffy rice.

NOTES:

- Many recipes for Picadillo call for cooking it just before serving, but I prefer to cook it ahead and allow time for the flavors to develop, then reheat just prior to serving.

- If the ground beef you purchase is not lean, cook it in a separate pan. Then drain off the grease through a colander before you add the beef to the recipe. Also, add a beef bouillon cube or two to compensate for any beef flavor lost when draining off the fat.

Here's another dish that's quite popular with those who visit the Cuban restaurants in Key West. In English, it's known as Spanish style Chicken with Rice. However, on the Spanish language menus, it's called...

Arroz con Pollo

INGREDIENTS (serves 6 to 8)

2	3-Pound	Frying chickens, cut up into serving sized pieces (*1)
6	Tbsps.	Olive oil
2	Medium	Onions, diced
2	Cloves	Garlic, diced
2		Green bell peppers, stem and seeds removed, diced
2	Cups	Tomatoes, peeled, seeded and chopped, or 1 can (16 ounces), drained
3	Cups	Chicken stock
2	Cups	Rice
1		Bay leaf
1	Tbsp.	Salt
1	Tsp.	Black pepper, freshly ground
1/2	Tsp.	Saffron
1	Cup	Fresh peas, or frozen peas, thawed

ARROZ CON POLLO (continued)

DIRECTIONS

- In a large Dutch oven, brown the chicken in oil for 10 minutes. Remove chicken and reserve.

- Add the onion, garlic and peppers to the Dutch oven and saute gently for about 5 minutes.

- Stir in the tomatoes, chicken stock, rice, bay leaf, salt and pepper. Stir in the saffron (*2) and bring the mixture to a boil.

- Return the chicken to the Dutch oven, cover tightly, and place in a preheated 350° oven for 10 minutes.

- Mix in peas, decorate with pimiento, cover and cook 15 minutes longer, or until chicken and rice are cooked.

NOTES

*1 Don't forget to save the chicken necks...use them to catch blue crabs!

*2 In Key West many cooks use a condiment called BIJOL, which is quite inexpensive, yet gives rice the same golden color as saffron.

Ropa Vieja (means "Old Clothes")

INGREDIENTS (serves 6)

2	Pounds	Beef flank steak, cut into 2" cubes
3	Medium	Onions, coarsely chopped
7	Cloves	Garlic, finely diced
3		Green bell peppers, stem and seeds removed, coarsely chopped
6		Bay leaves
1/2	Cup	Vinegar
1/4	Tsp.	Salt
1/8	Tsp.	Black pepper, freshly ground
2	Tbsps.	Olive oil
1	Can	Tomato paste (6 ounces)
		Pimiento strips
		Pimiento stuffed olives, sliced

DIRECTIONS

- In a large Dutch oven, brown the flank steak together with one onion and one half the garlic.

- Add one green pepper, 3 bay leaves, 1/4 cup of the vinegar, salt, pepper and water to cover. Simmer until meat is tender, about 1 1/2 hours.

- Skim the foam. Remove the meat and allow to cool, then strip into small pieces. Reserve cooking broth.

- Saute remaining onions, garlic and peppers in olive oil until tender. Add meat, remaining bay leaves, vinegar and 1/4 cup of reserved broth.

- Simmer until liquid is absorbed. Remove bay leaves and stir in the tomato paste.

- Serve on a platter, garnished with pimiento strips and slices of stuffed olives.

So…you've got a gang of black beans left over from your Cuban roast pork dinner. Never fear…for here's the recipe to turn those leftover beans into a delightful pot of…

Old Fashioned Black Bean Soup

INGREDIENTS (serves 6)

3	Tbsps.	Bacon drippings
2	Cloves	Garlic, minced
1	Medium	Onion, diced (or left over rings of onions used as garnish on Cuban Roast Pork)
1	Stalk	Celery, coarsely diced
1	Medium	Carrot, coarsely diced
		Leftover pork bones
4	Cups	Water
2	Medium	Tomatoes (or one 16 ounce can), peeled cored, seeded and chopped
3/4	Tsp.	Oregano
1/2	Tsp.	Cayenne pepper
1/4	Tsp.	Thyme
4	Cups	Cooked black beans (or two 16 ounce cans)
2	Tsps.	Salt
1/8	Tsp.	Black pepper, freshly ground
1/2	Cup	Dry sherry
2		Eggs, hard cooked

DIRECTIONS

• Heat bacon drippings in a 4 quart pan. Add garlic, onion, celery and carrot. Stir-fry over moderate heat for 8 to 10 minutes, until golden.

• Add the left-over bones and 4 cups of water, the tomatoes, oregano, cayenne and thyme. Cover and simmer gently for one hour.

- Strain stock through a sieve into a mixing bowl.
  Chill until any fat congeals on top of bowl. Remove
  fat and discard.

- Combine stock and beans. Simmer for about 1 1/2
  to 2 hours, until beans are mushy. Puree beans by
  pressing through a sieve. (This step is optional.)

- Return to pan and add salt, pepper and sherry.
  Heat, stirring frequently, for 5 to 10 minutes to
  blend flavors. Taste and adjust seasonings if desired.

- Peel the eggs, sieve the yolks and mince the whites.

- Ladle soup into large bowls, sprinkle with egg yolk
  and whites and serve.

*Many Cuban restaurants and sandwich shops sell Bollos.
These small fritters are made from ground beans and
can be eaten alone as a snack or as a vegetable with a meal.*

Bollos

INGREDIENTS (makes about 2 dozen)

2	Cups	Black eyed beans (1 pound)
1/2	Tsp.	Salt
1/4	Tsp.	Garlic powder
1/8	Tsp.	Cayenne pepper
		Vegetable oil, for frying

DIRECTIONS

- Cover beans with water and soak overnight. In the morning, carefully peel the shells from the beans.

- Using a fine blade in your grinder, grind the beans several times. It should look like mushy cornmeal.

- Add the salt, garlic powder and pepper and a little water. Beat the batter with a spoon...the longer the better, until it's the consistency of cake batter.

- Heat oil for frying, 2 inches deep in a fryer, to 375°.

- Shape the batter into small balls with a teaspoon. When batter is of the correct consistency, it will hold to the spoon.

- Drop Bollos into the hot oil, a few at a time, and deep fry for 3 to 4 minutes, until golden brown.

- Drain on paper towels. Break one open to test for doneness. Taste and adjust seasonings, if desired.

Doria Valdez
Key West

Bolichi (Cuban Style Pot Roast)

INGREDIENTS (serves 4)

1		Bolichi roast (eye of round roast, about 2 pounds)
1	Cup	Ham, chopped
3		Hard cooked eggs, chopped
1	Tsp.	Salt
1/2	Tsp.	Black pepper, freshly ground
3	Cloves	Garlic, sliced
3	Tbsps.	Olive oil
1	Can	Tomato sauce (8 ounces)
1	Tbsp.	Worcestershire sauce
2	Medium	Onions, chopped
1	Tsp.	Comino (Cumin) seeds
2		Bay leaves

DIRECTIONS

- Cut a large pocket from end to end of roast. Combine the chopped ham and eggs, and fill the pocket with this mixture.

- Cut numerous slits around outside of roast and insert garlic slices.

- In a large, deep pan with a tight cover, brown roast on all sides in olive oil.

- Add tomato sauce, Worcestershire sauce, onions, comino and bay leaves.

- Cover and cook over low heat for 45 minutes per pound. Remove bay leaves before serving.

Yellow Rice with Pork and Okra

INGREDIENTS (serves 6)

6	Medium	Pork chops, deboned and cut into 1/2 inch pieces
1/2	Cup	Salad oil
1	Large	Onion, diced
1	Medium	Green bell pepper, stem and seeds removed, diced
1	Medium	Tomato, seeds removed, diced
4	Cloves	Garlic, finely diced
1/2	Pound	Okra, cut into 1/2 inch rings
2 1/2	Cups	Water
2	Tsps.	Salt
1/4	Tsp.	BIJOL (yellow coloring)
2	Cups	Rice
1	Ounce	Vinegar

DIRECTIONS

- In a Dutch oven, fry the pork pieces in oil for about 10 minutes at medium heat.

- Add the onion, pepper, tomato and garlic. Fry for about 5 minutes.

- Add okra, water, salt and BIJOL. Boil for 5 minutes.

- Add rice and boil for 5 minutes at high heat. Lower heat, cover tightly, and simmer gently for 25 minutes.

- Add vinegar, recover, and wait 5 minutes more. Remove from stove and serve.

Martha Menendez
Key West Citizen
Cooking Contest

Conch

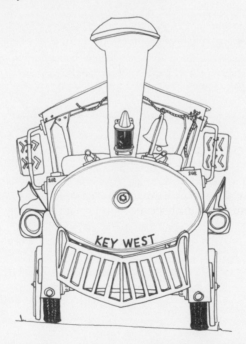

...An Introduction

We had been out fishing with Bud Kennedy and his wife
Mickey on the "We Five," captained by Dick Farcus.
After catching our share of bull dolphin (dorado), the
gals suggested that enough tossing about was enough, so
we headed toward calmer waters for lunch.

With a knowing smile on his face, Captain Dick anchored
his boat in waters about 3 feet deep. The mate promptly
jumped overboard, but within seconds had surfaced and
was passing us a conch (pronounced "konk").

We immediately donned snorkeling masks and joined the
mate. Within a short time, we had a catch of more than
a dozen conchs.

As the "We Five" made its way back to the dock at Geiger
Key, Captain Dick told us a little about Conch and how
Key West came to be called "The Conch Republic."

Conch is a spiral shelled gastropod which is found off
the coasts of Florida, the Gulf coasts and in the West
Indies. The meat is used for food and the shells, with
their beautiful shape and lovely pink interior, are
popular as decorations and for use as a "trumpet."
Conchs are so popular in Key West that natives are
actually called "Conchs".

Years ago, on April 18, 1982, the United States
Border Patrol established a road block at the head of
the only highway into and out of the Florida Keys. The
purpose of the road block was to catch illegal aliens.
For the first time in U.S. history, an entire section
of the country was officially treated as a foreign land.
Returning travelers were required to prove United States
citizenship and subjected to forced searches.

In retaliation, on April 23, 1982, the island of Key
West, in a mock ceremony, declared its independence from
the United States. What did the Key Westers call their
new nation? Naturally enough...they called it "The
Conch Republic."

REMOVING THE CONCH FROM ITS SHELL

There are several popular methods utilized in the Keys to remove the conch from its shell.

- Give them the cold treatment: Put them in a freezer, or pack them in ice, or place them in a cold refrigerator. After 48 hours, place the shells in water until thawed. The animal can then be easily removed.

- Give them a hot foot: Boil them as follows:
  1) Scrub the conch shell well under cold running water. (When found, ours were covered with green sea growth.)
  2) Place in a large heavy kettle.
  3) Cover with boiling water, add 1 tablespoon of salt and 1/4 cup of lemon juice.
  4) Cover and boil for 3 minutes, just until conch retreats into shell
  5) Drain in a colander under cold running water until easy to handle
  6) Pry the meat from the shell with a strong long-tined fork.

- Cut the muscle loose: Place the conch on a counter with the opening down. Start at the tip of the spiral, measure along it for two inches. using an ice pick and a hammer, puncture the shell at this point. Stick the ice pick inside the hole and rotate it to pry the muscle free. Hold the shell up, with the open end down, and the conch will slowly drop out, perhaps assisted with the ice pick.

- Hang them: Prepare a noose and hang it from a tree. Suspend a conch in the noose with the opening facing downward. Hook a fish hook into the foot and to the hook attach a short line and a one pound weight. After a short time the conch will relax and become fully extended from the shell. At this point you can sneak up on him and cut him loose.

TO CLEAN CONCH

Once you've got the conch out of the shell, the inedible portions must be removed. Cut away the eyes, the orange mantle (tightly curled tip) and the darker meat next to the foot (or operculum). Next, devein the conch. To skin, score around the foot and vertically through the skin. Peel away the strips of skin. Wash the remaining pure white meat thoroughly.

TO PURCHASE CONCH MEAT

Conch meat can now be purchased frozen (whole or ground) in some gourmet and specialty food markets.

TO TENDERIZE (OR NOT)

In most of the cookbooks and articles I've read, the next step in the process is to tenderize the meat. Conch meat can be quite tough and rubbery...and tenderizing may be required. Following are two popular methods.

- Pound it with a mallet, a coke bottle, or the edge of a heavy plate to break up the tough membranes.

- Parboil it. Leave conch meat whole or slice it thin. Place in a saucepan and add water to cover. For each pint of water, add 1 tablespoon of lemon juice. Cover and simmer until tender, about 1 1/2 to 2 hours for sliced conch, and about 2 to 4 hours for whole. Drain well.

Based upon the conversations I've had, conch meat is not necessarily tough and rubbery. The method of removing the meat from the shell can influence its tenderness, as can the length of cooking time. The following appears to be a current consensus on the subject.

- If you purchase the conch from a specialty food market or a fish market...tenderizing is not required.

- If you grind the conch before using...tenderizing is not required.

- Conch meat is delicate and prolonged cooking tends to toughen it...add conch to your recipe at the last possible moment and give only a minimal amount of cooking.

- If you have removed the conch from the shell by boiling...it may well be tough and require pounding or simmering to tenderize.

- If you are going to simmer it for 1 1/2 to 4 hours to make it tender...the liquid in which it was cooked probably will taste better then the conch...so simmer it in a liquid you'll want to use in the recipe. See recipe for Court Bouillon.

ABALONE, CLAMS AND SCUNGILLI

Conch meat may also be substituted in most recipes which call for abalone, clam* and scungilli.

* You may now wish to run out and buy a copy of "The Clam Lover's Cookbook"...also by Yours Truly.

If absolutely fresh, conch can be marinated and eaten raw.

Marinated Conch

INGREDIENTS

4		Conch
2		Tomatoes, peeled, seeded and diced
1	Medium	Onion, finely diced
1		Green bell pepper, stem and seeds removed, finely diced
1	Stalk	Celery, finely diced (optional)
1/2	Cup	Lime juice
1/2	Tsp.	Salt
1/8	Tsp.	Black pepper, freshly ground
1/8	Tsp.	Cayenne pepper (optional)

DIRECTIONS

- Remove conch from shells and cut away unusable portions. Pound the muscle with the end of a plate to break up the tough membranes and soften it. Dice meat finely.

- Combine diced conch with remaining ingredients and mix well. Chill for 1 to 2 hours.

- Serve on lettuce leaves, or in avocado halves.

Cracked Conch

INGREDIENTS (serves 4)

4		Conchs
1/2	Cup	Lime juice
		Vegetable oil, for frying
2		Eggs, beaten
1/2	Cup	Flour
1/2	Cup	Dry bread crumbs
1/2	Tsp.	Garlic salt
1/4	Tsp.	Cayenne pepper
1/4	Tsp.	Basil

DIRECTIONS

• Remove conch from shells and cut away unusable portions. Pound the conch with a wooden mallet until it looks like lace.

• Marinate it in lime juice for several hours.

• Heat 1 inch of vegetable oil to 375°.

• Dip the meat into beaten eggs, then into flour, back into eggs, then into bread crumbs seasoned with garlic salt, Cayenne and basil.

• Fry in hot vegetable oil until crispy brown, about 4 to 5 minutes. Serve with wedges of Key lime.

Fried Conch

INGREDIENTS (serves 4)

4		Conchs
1	Cup	Cracker crumbs
1/2	Tsp.	Salt
1/8	Tsp.	Black pepper, freshly ground
		Shortening or salad oil, for frying
1		Egg, lightly beaten

DIRECTIONS

- Remove conch from shells and cut away unusable portions. Pound with the edge of a plate to break the tough membranes. Cut into 1/4 inch slices.

- Combine cracker crumbs, salt and pepper.

- Heat 1 inch of shortening to 375°.

- Dip conch slices in cracker crumbs, next into beaten eggs and then again into the cracker crumbs.

- Drop pieces into hot fat and fry until golden brown, about 4 to 5 minutes.

Conch in Marinara Sauce

INGREDIENTS (serves 4)

1 1/2	Pounds	Conch meat, thinly sliced
1	Tsp.	Salt
1	Quart	Water
3	Tbsps.	Olive oil
2	Cloves	Garlic, finely diced
1	Medium	Onion, finely diced
1	Stalk	Celery, finely diced
1	Can	Tomatoes (16 ounces)
2	Tbsps.	Tomato paste
1/2	Tsp.	Salt
1/2	Tsp.	Oregano
1/2	Tsp.	Basil
2		Bay leaves
1/2	Tsp.	Crushed red pepper
1/2	Pound	Linguini

DIRECTIONS

- Simmer the conch in salted water for 15 minutes. Drain.

- Put olive oil, conch, garlic, onion and celery in a skillet. Brown well.

- Add the tomatoes, tomato paste, salt, oregano, basil, bay leaves and red pepper. Simmer gently until conch is tender. Remove bay leaves.

- Cook the linguini 8 to 10 minutes, until al dente (just cooked). Drain.

- Toss linguini with half the conch marinara. Spoon the remainder over the linguini and serve.

Conch Republic Burgers

INGREDIENTS (makes 4)

6	Tbsps.	Flour
1	Tsp.	Baking powder
1/2	Tsp.	Salt
2		Eggs, beaten
1	Cup	Ground conch
2	Tbsps.	Onion, finely chopped
2	Tbsps.	Green bell pepper, finely chopped
1	Small	Hot pepper, finely chopped (optional)
4	Drops	Tabasco sauce
2	Tbsps.	Melted butter
1/4	Cup	Vegetable oil

DIRECTIONS

• Sift together the flour, baking powder and salt.
  Set aside.

• In a separate bowl, beat the eggs, add the ground
  conch, the onion, green and hot pepper, Tabasco
  sauce and melted butter.

• Add sifted dry ingredients, and mix thoroughly.
  Mixture will be thick but not firm.

• Heat vegetable oil in a large skillet and spoon the
  conch batter into the hot fat, forming 4 patties
  (either round or oval).

• Cook on medium-low heat until brown on bottom,
  about 4 to 5 minutes. Carefully turn and cook an
  additional 4-5 minutes until browned.

SERVING SUGGESTIONS

• If desired, melt cheese of your choice on top of
  burgers after they are turned.

CONCH REPUBLIC BURGERS (continued)

- Delicious when garnished with sauteed mushrooms and/or onions on top.

- Try serving them with tartar sauce and lime wedges.

Susan E. Mowery, Finalist
Key West Citizen
Cooking Contest

Conch Burgers

INGREDIENTS (serves 4 - 6)

2	Cups	Parboiled conch meat, finely ground
2	Cups	Soft white bread crumbs
2		Eggs, lightly beaten
1	Tbsp.	Worcestershire sauce
1/4	Tsp.	Tabasco sauce
1	Clove	Garlic, finely diced
1	Small	Onion, finely diced
1/4	Cup	Unsifted flour
3	Tbsps.	Butter (or bacon drippings)

DIRECTIONS

- In a mixing bowl, combine the conch meat, bread crumbs, eggs, Worcestershire sauce, Tabasco sauce, garlic and onion.

- Shape into six patties and dredge with flour.

- Heat butter in a large skillet over moderate heat. Brown patties, 3 to 4 minutes on each side.

- Serve hot with catsup or tartar sauce.

Here is the best recipe I've seen for Conch Fritters. It's based on a recipe which first appeared in the Miami Herald. To me, the best way to serve Conch Fritters is with a bowl of rich tomato-based Conch Chowder.

Conch Fritters

INGREDIENTS (serves 4-6)

1	Cup	Milk
1	Tsp.	Vinegar
1	Pound	Conch
1	Medium	Onion, quartered
1		Green bell pepper, stem and seeds removed,quartered
1	Rib	Celery
2	Cups	All purpose flour
1	Tbsp.	Baking powder
1	Tbsp.	Baking soda
1/2	Tsp.	Salt
1/4	Tsp.	Black pepper, freshly ground
2		Eggs, lightly beaten
1/2	Tsp.	Tabasco sauce
		Shortening (or cooking oil), for frying

DIRECTIONS

- Combine the milk and vinegar. Allow to sit for 15 minutes to sour.

- Grind together the conch, onion, green pepper and celery.

- In a large mixing bowl, mix together the flour, baking powder, baking soda, salt and pepper.

- Stir in the soured milk, the ground conch mixture, the eggs and the Tabasco sauce.

- In a deep fryer, heat shortening or cooking oil, 2 inches deep, to 375°.

CONCH FRITTERS (continued)

- Using a teaspoon or tablespoon, drop mixture into hot shortening, a few at a time and fry until golden brown, about 4 to 5 minutes.

- Drain fritters on paper towels. After cooking the first batch, break one open and test for doneness. Taste and add more salt or pepper to the batter, if desired.

- Continue making fritters until all batter has been used. Garnish with sprigs of parsley and lemon wedges. Serve hot with Conch Chowder or with Tartar Sauce and Seafood Cocktail Sauce.

VARIATION

- Use 1/2 of a green bell pepper and one Jalapeno pepper, stem and seeds removed. Reduce Tabasco sauce to 1/4 teaspoon.

Seafood Cocktail Sauce

INGREDIENTS (makes about 1 scant cup)

3/4	Cup	Catsup (or combination of catsup and chili sauce)
2	Tbsps.	Prepared horseradish, drained (or more. .. to taste)
1	Tbsp.	Lemon (or Key lime) juice
1/2	Tsp.	Salt (or celery salt)
1/8	Tsp.	Black pepper, freshly ground
1/2	Tsp.	Worcestershire sauce
1/8	Tsp.	Tabasco sauce (or Cayenne pepper)

DIRECTIONS

- Combine all ingredients in a plastic container. Cover and refrigerate until well chilled.

Tomato Based Conch Chowder

INGREDIENTS (makes about 5 quarts)

8	Large	Conchs (about 2 1/2 pounds of meat)
1/4	Pound	Salt pork (or bacon)
1	Medium	Onion, diced
2	Cups	Celery, diced
1/2	Cup	Green bell pepper, stem and seeds removed, diced
1	Can	Tomatoes (20 ounces)
2	Tsps.	Salt
3/4	Tsp.	Black pepper, freshly ground
1	Tsp.	Thyme
2	Cups	Potatoes, diced
1/2	Cup	Carrots, grated

DIRECTIONS

• Remove conch from shells and cut away unusable portions. Pound, with a wooden mallet, to soften then dice finely.

• Brown the salt pork, then drain off all but 2 table-spoons drippings. Saute the onion, celery and pepper for 15 minutes.

• Add the conch, tomatoes, salt, pepper, thyme and 2 quarts boiling water. Cook over low heat for 2 hours.

• Add potatoes and carrots. Cook for 20 minutes. Taste for seasoning. Serve hot.

VARIATIONS

• Omit potatoes and add one of the following just before serving:

1/2 cup pearl barley, cooked according to package directions
2 cups cooked rice

Milk Based Conch Chowder

INGREDIENTS (makes about 3 quarts)

1	Pound	Conch meat
5	Cups	Water
1	Tsp	Salt
1/8	Pound	Salt pork (or bacon), diced
1	Large	Onion, diced
4		Potatoes, diced
1/4	Tsp.	Black pepper, freshly ground
1	Pint	Milk

DIRECTIONS

- Pound the conch meat with a wooden mallet until tender.

- Place conch in a 4 quart saucepan. Add the water and salt. Cover and simmer for 1 hour.

- Remove conch and drain. Pass the conch meat through a food chopper and return to the liquid.

- Meanwhile, fry the salt pork in a skillet until fat flows freely. Remove crisp scraps and reserve.

- Add onion to fat and cook until light brown.

- Add onions, potatoes and pepper to saucepan containing chopped conch meat and stock. Cook for about 20 minutes, until potatoes are tender.

- Heat milk to the scalding point and add to chowder. Add reserved salt pork pieces. Taste and adjust seasonings. Serve hot.

Here's a great gourmet treat to have ready for those Northerners who drop in when the yellowtail are not biting.

Creamy Chilled Conch Chowder

INGREDIENTS (makes about 2 quarts)

2	Cups	Fresh (not frozen) conch, finely ground (about 1 pound)
1	Bottle	"Old Sour" (16 ounces)
4	Medium	Cucumbers, seeded, diced but not peeled
1	Clove	Garlic, finely diced
1	Dash	Tabasco sauce
1/4	Tsp.	Celery seed
1/8	Tsp.	Ground bay leaves
1/2	Tsp.	Dill weed
1/4	Tsp.	Rosemary
1/2	Tsp.	White pepper
3	Cups	Plain yogurt
1	Cup	Sour cream
		Parsley, for garnish

DIRECTIONS

- Place the conch meat in a bowl. Add "Old Sour" until conch meat is just covered.

- Cover bowl and refrigerate for five days, as the conch meat cooks. Stir about twice each day, and add more "Old Sour" if required.

- Place cucumbers and garlic in a sauce pan and cover with water. Simmer just until the cukes look glassy. Drain. Add the Tabasco sauce, celery seed, bay leaves, dill weed, rosemary and pepper. Chill.

- When cucumber mixture is cold, add the yogurt, sour cream and the marinated (and drained) conch meat. Refrigerate until ready to serve…and then sprinkle each serving with parsley.

SERVING SUGGESTIONS

- Serve in cups with Cuban bread slices fried in garlic butter.

- Serve in small cups garnished with herb flavored croutons, grated raw carrots, chopped scallions, alfalfa, sieved hard boiled eggs, thinly sliced green bell pepper or radishes.

- Halve an avocado, remove seed, sprinkle with lemon juice...and fill with chowder.

- Serve as a dip at your next buffet, jazzed up with horseradish to taste.

NOTE

- This dish keeps for at least a week tightly covered in the refrigerator.

Marian Witherspoon
3rd prize winner, Key West
Conch Chowder Cook-off

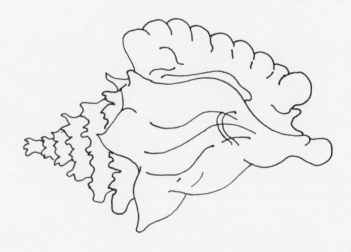

Blue Crabs

Many people who live in the Florida Keys have found a perfect use for chicken necks. Each time we serve chicken, the neck is saved and placed in a special sack in the freezer. After eight or ten have been collected...it's time to go a-crabbing. Before the necks are used they should be "seasoned." Just leave them out in the sun for about 24 hours, until they get good and "ripe"...then they're ready.

Our favorite spot is the second bridge on Boca Chica Road. We use what's called a star trap*, into which we tie a chicken neck**. The trap is lowered by a string down through the water, to rest open on the sandy bottom. The water flowing over the trap carries the flavor of the neck to our quarry. After a time, an unsuspecting crab will follow the scent and crawl onto the trap. At this point, we pull up on the string, closing the trap...and up comes a part of tonight's supper.

Now, I enjoy blue crab prepared in almost any manner. However, after spending more than ten years in Baltimore, I've developed just a slight bias toward some of the truly great ways they are prepared in Maryland. A few of these treasured recipes follow... as well as a few I've picked up while in the Keys.

* A star trap is basically a metal mesh frame, that when lowered and opened, looks like a four pointed star. When closed (hopefully with a nice fat crab inside) the trap resembles a four-sided pyramid.

** Canned catfood is also a terrific bait for crawfish or crabs. Punch holes in the can, tie or drop into the trap and the little critters will come running faster than a hungry cat.

Steamed Blue Crab

INGREDIENTS (serves 6 to 10)

1/2	Cup	Seafood seasoning
1/2	Cup	Salt, coarse grind
3	Cups	White vinegar
3	Cups	Water (or beer)
3	Dozen	Live blue crabs

DIRECTIONS

- Mix seafood seasoning, salt, vinegar and water.

- Put 1/2 of the crabs in a very large pot with a rack and a tight fitting lid.

- Pour 1/2 of the seasoning mix over top. Add the rest of the crabs and remaining mixture.

- Steam, covered, until crabs turn bright orange in color, about 20 minutes. Serve steaming hot.

NOTES

- Verify that the crab is alive when it goes into the pot. If the crab is dead. .. discard it.

- Many cooks like to keep the liquid and seasoning separate. This method allows the seasoning spice to stick to the crabs, rather than being washed off by the water and vinegar. If you'd like to try this method, proceed as follows:

  - Begin by pouring the water and vinegar into the bottom of the pot.

  - Insert the rack and add half of the crabs.

  - Mix together the seafood seasonings and salt. Sprinkle half of it over the crabs.

- Add the rest of the crabs and the remaining seasoning mixture.
- Steam, covered, until crabs turn bright orange in color, about 20 minutes. Serve steaming hot.

- In Maryland, the traditional way of serving steamed crabs is on a table covered with newspapers. Wooden mallets are used to break the claws and small paring knives are used to pry out the meat. Paper towels are used rather than napkins.

- The hot and spicy blend in which they are steamed does not affect the meat of the crab but as you suck out the meat from the various pieces of crab, some gets on your lips...and that spicy taste just begs for a frosty beer.

- Incidentally, if there are kids or ladies in the crowd who don't take to the spice mix, just rinse it off... the meat inside will be deliciously sweet.

This is a good way to use the claw meat from blue crabs.

Crab Meat Dip

INGREDIENTS (makes about 4 cups)

1/2	Pound	Crab meat
1/2	Cup	Celery, diced fine
1/2	Cup	Onion, diced fine
2	Ounces	Cream cheese, softened
3/4	Cup	Mayonnaise
1/2	Tsp.	Old Bay seafood seasoning mix

DIRECTIONS

- Pick over the crab meat to remove any bits of shell or cartilage. Add the celery and onion.

- Blend together the cream cheese, mayonnaise and seafood seasoning. Stir into the crab meat mixture. If too dry, add a bit more mayonnaise.

- Serve chilled with crackers.

NOTES

- To make the dish more attractive, substitute green onions with tops and add 1 tablespoon finely diced pimiento.

- If spicier flavor is desired, add more Old Bay or a pinch of garlic powder.

- If serving outdoors in a sunny area, place the serving bowl in a larger bowl of cracked ice.

Toni Murray
Key West

Recently, while visiting Ft. Lauderdale, Florida, we ate at "The Rustic Inn", where they are justifiably famous for the following dish. They won't tell you the recipe but after lots of (very enjoyable) experimentation, we have come up with the following.

Garlic Crabs

INGREDIENTS (serves 4)

6	Pounds	Blue crabs, apron and back shells removed, stomach and lungs removed, broken in half down the middle and rinsed under cold running water
2	Cups	Olive (or vegetable) oil
4	Buds	Garlic (not cloves), peeled and coarsely chopped
4	Tsps.	White pepper

DIRECTIONS

• Pour one cup of water in the bottom of a wok. Place crabs in a steamer and place steamer in the wok. Over high heat, steam the crabs for about 5 minutes, until they turn red.

• Discard the water from the steamer. Add the oil, garlic and white pepper to the wok and heat, over medium heat. Stir to thoroughly blend ingredients.

• Add crabs and toss to thoroughly coat with garlic oil. Lift crabs out of wok with tongs or a slotted spoon and place in a serving bowl.

• Serve with a wooden mallet to break claws and lots of napkins. This dish is eaten with your fingers.

*Crab cakes have got to be one of the world's greatest tasting treats.
I learned to love them while living in Baltimore a few years back.
They are delicious served either as a main course or as a sandwich
between two saltine crackers. Now I'm living in the Florida Keys
and blue crabs are just waiting to be caught off a nearby bridge.
Who says you have to die to go to Heaven!*

Crab Cakes

INGREDIENTS (makes 6 cakes)

1	Pound	Crab meat (from blue crabs)
1	Cup	Italian-seasoned bread crumbs
1	Large	Egg, lightly beaten
1/4	Cup	Mayonnaise
1/2	Tsp.	Salt
1/2	Tsp.	Black pepper, freshly ground
1	Tsp.	Worcestershire sauce
1	Tsp.	Dry mustard
		Butter or oil (for frying)

DIRECTIONS

• Carefully pick over the crab meat to assure that no
pieces of shell remain.

• In a mixing bowl, combine the bread crumbs, egg,
mayonnaise, salt, pepper, Worcestershire sauce and
mustard. Add crab meat last and mix thoroughly.
If mixture seems too dry, add a little more mayonnaise.

• Shape into six cakes and refrigerate until meal time.

• Fry in just enough fat to prevent sticking until
browned, about 5 minutes on each side. As an
alternative, they can be deep fried until browned,
about 2 to 3 minutes.

Several years ago some friends took me out to supper in Mobile, Alabama. I don' t remember what the restaurant was named, or what we had for the main course...but I surely do remember the appetizers. There were two...both featuring blue crab and both were extraordinary. The first was called "Caribe Crab" and the second was "Fried Crab Fingers".

Caribe Crab

INGREDIENTS (serves 2)

1	Pound	Lump blue crab meat
1	Small	Onion, grated
2	Tbsps.	Lime juice (1/2 lime)
1/4	Tsp.	Salt
1/8	Tsp.	Black pepper, freshly ground

DIRECTIONS

- Carefully pick over the crab meat to assure that all pieces of cartilage or shell has been removed.

- Add remaining ingredients and stir lightly to mix. Divide between two bowls and serve.

NOTE

- The portions were really generous. The flavoring was as subtle as could be...and they didn't dress it up with a bed of lettuce. Just a bowl of crab meat... but each bite was more delicious than its predecessor.

- My friend, Toni, advised me that when she's had this dish, crackers were served with it. Could be, but to me, it's perfect just as it is.

As I finished eating that bowl of succulent crab, I was confident that nothing could equal it. But my hosts just smiled knowingly. Out came a pound of breaded, deep fried crab fingers. Do you know how many crab fingers there are to a pound? Neither do I...for they disappeared much too fast to get a count. Dipped in a tangy cocktail sauce, they were out-of-this-world delicious!

Deep-fried Crab Fingers

INGREDIENTS (serves 4)

1	Pound	Blue crab fingers
2		Eggs, lightly beaten
1	Cup	Dried bread crumbs
1/4	Tsp.	Salt
1/8	Tsp.	Black pepper, freshly ground
		Vegetable oil (for frying)
		Cocktail sauce (recipe follows)

DIRECTIONS

• Crab fingers are actually the last section of each claw, the part containing the pincers. After cooking the whole crab, remove this section at the first joint. Remove shell by placing a knife on the shell near the pincer and tapping it with a kitchen hammer until it cracks. Gently pull off the shell to reveal... a tasty finger shaped morsel of crab. The pincers are left intact for use as a handle.

• Hold each finger by the pincer, dip first into the beaten egg and then roll in a mixture of bread crumbs, salt and pepper. Tap slightly to remove any excess bread crumbs.

• Heat oil in a skillet or deep fryer at 360°. Drop the fingers, a few at a time, into the hot fat and fry until golden brown, about 3 to 4 minutes.

• Drain on paper towels. Place on a paper towel lined baking dish. Hold, in a 200 degree oven, until all fingers are fried.

• Serve with a tangy seafood cocktail sauce.

Stone Crabs

Stone Crabs ... An Introduction

The meat from the claws of stone crabs is another justifiably famous Florida Keys seafood. One of the first things I did after arriving in the Keys was to get a small boat, an outboard motor, some fishing gear, five stone crab traps and a license from the State to catch them.

My fishing companion was usually a guy named Nick Megura (famed as a triple ace in the Second World War) who now spends summers in Bridgeport, Connecticut, and winters in the Keys.

Nick and I, we'd obtain some fish heads from friends as they cleaned their fish. Then we'd bait the crab traps with the heads and set them out. About two days later we'd go fishing. After our day of fishing, and on the way back in to our docks, we'd stop at the traps and usually find an average of one crab in each. Now the fun begins. (The claws on a stone crab can be almost as large as the body. As a fisherman, you are allowed to break off and keep the claws, but the body has to be returned to the ocean, where after about a year, he will grow new claws.)

Here is our method for obtaining those prized claws: After the crab trap is open, you offer the crab the end of a stick about 18 inches long...which he grabs. Lifting him up with the stick, allow him to grab the wooden top of the trap with his free claw. Now that both claws are occupied, sneak up behind him and quickly grab one claw in each hand, keeping your hands close to the body of the crab. Quickly twist and break one claw off, drop it in the boat...grab the body with your free hand and then twist the other claw off. Toss the crab overboard, toss the two claws in a bucket, bait the trap with one or two small fish and drop the trap overboard. (We'd be back two days later with the heads from the larger fish in our catch to rebait the traps...and keep the cycle going.)

I know how to remove stone crab claws because I've watched it being done a hundred times. My friend Nick does it, my girlfriend Agnes does it...but not me! Those claws look like they could easily remove a finger and hell, I'm an author... I need my fingers to write.

Let me tell you a story about Nick. As I've said, we'd frequently go fishing together. On this particular day, after we'd caught a cooler full of fish, we'd pulled in our stone crab traps. For our trouble we were rewarded with about six stone crab claws and a bonus of one large blue crab. As there wasn't enough crab to feed us both, I offered them to Nick, who took them home and tossed them into his sink.

Later, at supper time, he reached into the sink for the crab claws, and…surprise!…the blue crab grabbed him good, right on the finger. He jumped back and the crab got him in the stomach with his other claw.
Nick was now standing there, that crab holding him in two places. Fortunately, with his free hand he was able to grab the crab, break off one of the offending claws and ultimately end the contest. But he surely did sport a couple of good scratches for a few days.

Stone Crab Claws are Purchased Precooked

Crabs, as they grow, periodically outgrow and then shed their shells (i.e., soft shell crabs). They quickly form a larger shell around them…into which they continue growing. During this period of growth the claws of the stone crab are not completely filled with meat…which brings us to the reason why the stone crabs you purchase in the seafood market have already been cooked.

When a stone crabber brings his catch to the seafood wholesaler, the claws are immediately immersed in a pot of hot boiling water. Those claws that float (called 'lights') are skimmed off after cooking and returned to the crabber. The remainder, which are heavy with meat, are purchased by the wholesaler...and eventually sold to us guys.

Occasionally, at the Sunday Flea Market in Key West, you'll find a man selling stone crab claws for about half the seafood market price. His sign doesn't say so...but he will quickly admit that what he's selling are 'lights'. So...for half the price...you must break open twice as many shells to get the same amount of meat.

Get yourself ready for one of the most delicious dishes in the world.

Hot Stone Crab Claws with Melted Butter

- Allow about 4 claws per serving.

- Boil the crab claws in salted water for about 20 minutes.

- Remove claws from water and place on a folded cloth. Crack each of the 3 sections with a wooden mallet. (As the shell is 1/8 inch or more in thickness, a good hard crack is often required.)

- Serve with melted butter.

Cold Stone Crab Claws with Mustard Sauce

- Follow the steps described above for cooking and cracking the claw.

- Drain and chill. Arrange about 4 claws for each serving.

- Serve with Mustard Sauce...two recipes follow.

*Joe's Stone Crab Restaurant, a famous Miami establishment, has been in
the same location since 1913. Among other dishes, they are famous for
stone crab claws. Here's the sauce they serve with stone crab.*

Joe's Stone Crab Mustard Sauce

INGREDIENTS (makes 3/4 cup sauce)

1/2	Cup	Mayonnaise
1	Tbsp.	Steak sauce
1	Tbsp.	Worcestershire sauce
1	Tbsp.	Colman's dry English mustard
1/4	Cup	Light cream

DIRECTIONS

* In a small mixing bowl, combine all ingredients except the cream
  and beat slowly. Gradually, while beating constantly, add the
  cream. Beat at slow speed until it thickens and becomes smooth
  and creamy.

Here's another mustard sauce you may wish to try.

Blender Mustard Sauce

INGREDIENTS (makes about 2 cups)

1		Whole egg
2	Tsps.	White wine vinegar
1/4	Tsp.	Salt
2	Tsps.	Dry mustard
2/3	Cup	Vegetable oil
1/3	Cup	Olive oil
1	Tbsp.	Dijon style mustard

DIRECTIONS

* Place the egg, vinegar, salt and 1 teaspoon of the
  dry mustard in the blender container.

* Run at high speed, slowly dribbling in a mixture of vegetable
  and olive oil until sauce begins to thicken. Turn off machine
  periodically and scrape down the sides with a rubber spatula.

- In a separate dish combine the Dijon style mustard with the remaining dry mustard.

- When the sauce is slightly thickened, add the mustard mixture.

- Continue to blend, adding oil until sauce is very thick.

I was amazed when Vivian told me that she made the following salad with 50% potatoes and 50% crab meat (or crawfish). It gives a person an appreciation of one of the real advantages of living in an environment where normally expensive ingredients are in abundant supply.

Crab-Potato Salad

INGREDIENTS (serves 6 to 8)

4	Cups	Cooked stone crab meat, cartilage removed, lightly flaked with a fork
6	Medium	Potatoes, boiled, chilled, peeled and cubed
4		Eggs, hard cooked, chilled, peeled and diced
1/2	Medium	Green bell pepper, stem and seeds removed, finely diced
1	Medium	Onion, finely diced
2	Ribs	Celery, finely diced
2	Cups	Mayonnaise
1/4	Cup	Sweet pickle relish
1	Tbsp.	Salt
1/2	Tsp.	Black pepper, freshly ground
		Lettuce

DIRECTIONS

- Combine all ingredients except lettuce and chill for several hours. Serve as is or in crisp lettuce cups.

VARIATION

- Substitute crawfish (Florida lobster), cut into bite sized pieces.

Vivian Daniels
Marathon, Florida

Crawfish (Florida Lobster)

Crawfish...An Introduction

Crawfish (not to be confused with crayfish) is the local name for Florida lobsters. Unlike the Maine or northern lobster, they have no claws. They are actual spiny (or rock) lobsters and are recognized by the many prominent spines on their body and legs, as well as two long, slender antennae.

I spoke to my good friend Jim Hardee, who lives on Bay Point, about commercial crawfish fishing. (He's also the man you'll want to see if your outboard motor breaks down.)

He advised me that the season for catching them runs from the end of July through the beginning of April. To fish for crawfish using traps, a license is required. The State then assigns you a color code for your buoys and issues you a number. The color code and number must appear on each of your buoys and conspicuously on the boat you use to pull your traps. (That way the Florida Marine Patrol can fly over and verify that all is OK.)

Most commercial crawfishermen use rectangular traps constructed of wooden slats. Before being used the traps are dipped in used crankcase oil to protect against wood worms. They may be baited with fish heads, cowhide or even left empty. (Apparently, even empty traps will catch crawfish because the critters crawl into them to seek refuge.) A strong line is then attached to each trap, as well as your color coded buoy...and they are lowered off your boat into those spots where you hope crawfish reside. The traps then lie on the ocean bottom waiting for those succulent crawfish to come forth.

Once you've caught the crawfish, there are two methods of measuring your catch to see if they are large enough to keep.

- Carapace measure: From between the eyes to the back of head shell...must be three inches.

- Tail measure: From beginning of the tail to tip of flippers...must be 5 1/2 inches.

It's illegal to have a "short" (undersized crawfish) in your possession unless you are licensed. If licensed, you are permitted to have "shorts" in your boat while pulling your "pots" (traps), but even with your license you're not allowed to bring them back to your dock.

About three weeks after you start using your traps the crank case oil begins to wear off and the crawfish stop being attracted to it. The solution is to drop a couple of live "shorts" into the trap. This attracts the big crawfish.

Another type of trap is called the barrel trap. To make one, take a 55 gallon barrel and remove one end. Turn the barrel on its side, jump up and down on it until it's almost flattened and the open end or "mouth" is about 6 inches by 4 feet. Next take an axe and make about 50 cuts all over it. Tie a line and your official buoy to it and it's ready to go.

If you don't have a commercial license, you can still use a barrel trap, as long as you don't put a line or buoy on it…and as long as you don't pull it into your boat. This means that you can swim down to it, "tickle" the crawfish out and into a net, or reach in and grab him. He can't bite you but the spine will stick you if you're not careful. If you like diving, this method may be for you. However, it's illegal for a diver to use a spear gun, gig, or in any other way puncture a crawfish shell to catch him.

Here's another crawfishing method that might appeal to you. Take a small boat and mount a light above it up on a pole. Go out at night into areas where the water isn't too deep. With the light you'll be able to see the crawfish (they come out to feed at night.) Drop a "bully" net (a bully net is a cone shaped net mounted onto a hoop at the end of a pole) over the crawfish. If you're lucky, he will react by swimming up into the net—and you've got him.

You say you don't have a "bully" net and still want to catch some crawfish. OK…here's a unique way of catching them, using just your wife's rag mop. When you see a crawfish in shallow water, drop the mop on top of him, holding on to the handle. Twist it a bit and the antennae and spines become entangled in the mop. Pull him into your boat and untangle the mop carefully from the spine.

I also talked to Jan Harris, who lives near me here in Seaside Resort, and he added to my information on the subject. He informed me that, without a commercial license, the limit on crawfish per person per day is six.

Jan catches his crawfish while snorkeling. He carries a pole (with a net at the end) and wears a PVC (polyvinyl-chloride) glove in case he has to grab one. He is also a spear fisherman and has that equipment. If possible, he carries a piece of squid...or better...octopus. Apparently, these are the crawfish's deadly enemies. When he takes a spear with a piece of either of these baits tied to the tip and sticks it into a hole or cavity in which crawfish are hiding, they quickly retreat out into his waiting net.

Jan told me his "crawfish philosophy." He catches all the crawfish that he and his lovely wife, Glenda, wish to eat. When people come to visit, he will feed them all the crawfish they desire. However...he gives none as gifts and he gives none to visitors to take home. His feeling is that our crawfish are a limited resource and if he freely gave away what he caught, not only would he be busy full time, but he would quickly deplete the "stock" in his favorite fishing areas. I like his philosophy.

To Buy and Store

- Whole crawfish will range in size from about one to two pounds. Allow one small or one-half of a large crawfish per serving. Store live crawfish in the refrigerator, covered with damp paper towels. Use within twelve hours.

- If using frozen lobster tail, plan on six to eight ounces for each serving.

To Simmer Crawfish

- If crawfish are live, rinse them off in cold water. If you have purchased frozen tails, either thaw them in the refrigerator or in cold water.

- Pour enough water in a large pan to generously cover the crawfish. Add two teaspoons of salt (optional) for each quart of water.

- Bring the water to a boil over high heat. Add the crawfish. Plunge live crawfish head first into the water and tuck crawfish tail under to prevent muscle reflex which could splash boiling water.

- Cover the pan. When the water resumes boiling, reduce heat and simmer until done.

  Whole . . . . .1 to 1 1/2 pounds - 12 to 15 minutes
                  1 1/2 to 2 pounds - 15 to 18 minutes
  Tails . . . . . . .2 to 4 ounces - 3 to 5 minutes
                     4 to 6 ounces - 5 to 7 minutes
                     6 to 8 ounces - 7 to 9 minutes

  The flesh of crawfish turns from translucent to opaque when cooked. To test for doneness, cut into the center of the tail.

- When done, remove crawfish at once and immerse briefly in cold water to stop cooking.

To Steam Crawfish

- If crawfish are live, rinse them off in cold water. If you have purchased frozen tails, either thaw them in the refrigerator or in cold water.

- You'll need a steamer or large pan with a rack inside at least two inches above bottom.

- Pour one inch of water into the pan and bring to a boil on high heat.

- Set the crawfish (up to five pounds) on the rack and cover the pan. When the pan fills with steam and it begins to escape from under the lid, reduce heat to medium and cook until done.

```
Whole  . . . . .1 to I 1/2 pounds - 12 to 15 minutes
               1 1/2 to 2 pounds - 15 to 18 minutes
Tails  . . . . . . .2 to 4 ounces - 3 to 5 minutes
               4 to 6 ounces - 5 to 7 minutes
               6 to 8 ounces - 7 to 9 minutes
```

The flesh of crawfish turns from translucent to opaque when cooked. To test for doneness, cut into the center of the tail.

- When done, remove crawfish immediately and immerse briefly in cold water to stop cooking.

To Serve and Eat

- Twist off the tail of whole crawfish where it joins the body. Twist off and discard the tail flippers.

- Push a fork deep into the large end of tail and gently pull the meat out in one piece, or cut away the under shell with scissors to remove meat.

- Carefully remove and discard the sand vein which runs the length of the tail.

- Serve with melted butter (when served hot), or with mayonnaise (if served chilled).

- Once cooked, it's best to eat it the same day. Don't keep it more than two days.

Crawfish and Olive En Brochette

INGREDIENTS (serves 6)

1 1/2	Pounds	Frozen crawfish tails
1/4	Cup	French dressing
1/2	Cup	Chili sauce
3/4	Tsp.	Salt
1/8	Tsp.	Black pepper, freshly ground
1/8	Tsp.	Garlic powder
24		Stuffed olives

DIRECTIONS

- Thaw the crawfish tails. Remove meat from shells and cut into one inch pieces.

- In a small jar, combine the French dressing, chili sauce, salt, pepper and garlic. Cover and shake the marinade well.

- Place crawfish pieces in a small mixing bowl and pour marinade over them. Marinate for 15 minutes.

- Alternate crawfish pieces and olives on 6 skewers, 7 1/2 inches each. Place skewers across a baking pan 10 X 6 X 1 1/2 inches.

- Bake, in a moderate 350° oven, for 20 to 25 minutes.

NOTES AND VARIATIONS

- Baste once during cooking with extra sauce.

- Feel free to add mushroom caps, cherry tomatoes, green bell pepper or onion pieces.

- Rather cook it on your charcoal grill? Go ahead... you'll love it that way too.

Crawfish Enchilada

INGREDIENTS (serves 4)

4	Slices	Salt pork (or bacon), diced
2	Large	Onions, diced
4	Ribs	Celery, diced
1	Large	Green bell pepper, stem and seeds removed, diced
2	Cloves	Garlic, finely diced
2	Cans	Tomato juice (12 ounces each)
2	Cans	Whole tomatoes (12 ounces each)
1	Tsp.	Worcestershire sauce
1	Quart	Water
2		Bay leaves
1/2	Tsp.	Salt
1/4	Tsp.	Black pepper, freshly ground
1/8	Tsp.	Ground red pepper
6		Crawfish tails, cooked, meat removed and cubed

DIRECTIONS

- In a large pot, saute the salt pork until lightly brown and crisp. Remove with a slotted spoon and drain on paper towels.

- Add the onion, celery, pepper and garlic. Saute vegetables until soft and lightly browned.

- Add tomato juice, tomatoes, Worcestershire sauce, water, bay leaves, salt and the black and red pepper. Simmer for 25 to 30 minutes.

- Add crawfish and pork. Cook for 10 minutes longer. Remove bay leaves and check seasonings. Serve over hot fluffy cooked rice.

Crawfish Stuffed with Stone Crab

INGREDIENTS (serves 4)

4	Ounces	Butter (1 stick)
2	Large	Onions, diced
1	Cup	Celery, diced
1	Large	Green bell pepper, stem and seeds removed, diced
3	Cups	Cooked stone crab meat, any cartilage removed, lightly flaked with a fork
1	Package	Pepperidge Farm Herb Seasoned Stuffing Water
8		Live crawfish
4	Tbsps.	Butter, melted

DIRECTIONS

• Melt the butter in a large frying pan or Dutch oven Add onion, celery and green pepper. Saute until onion is transparent, about 3 to 4 minutes.

• Add the stone crab meat and continue sauteing the mixture for 3 minutes.

• Remove from heat and stir in the herbal dressing. Add just enough water so that the mixture will hold together.

• Place each crawfish "face" down on a cutting board. Kill the crawfish by inserting a sharp knife into joint where tail and body come together, to cut the spinal cord.

• Place crawfish on its back and with a sharp knife make a deep incision at the mouth. With a quick cut, split each crawfish lengthwise to end of tail.

• Open cavity and remove stomach, intestinal vein (running the length of body), liver and coral. Save the liver and coral if you wish to add them to the dressing.

CRAWFISH STUFFED WITH STONE CRAB (continued)

- Stuff the head section with the stone crab stuffing
  mixture, mounding the stuffing up slightly. Arrange
  side by side, cut side up, in a large shallow roasting
  pan. Brush exposed tail section generously with
  melted butter.

- Bake, in a preheated 350° oven, for 25 to 30 minutes.
  Baste often with pan juices. Sprinkle with salt and
  freshly ground black pepper and serve at once, 2
  crawfish per person.

Stone Crab Claw Patties

- Shape any leftover dressing into patties, about
  3 inches round and 1 inch thick. Refrigerate
  or freeze the patties to be fried in butter at
  another meal.

Vivian Daniels
Marathon, Florida

Shrimp

One of Key West's major businesses is shrimp fishing. It's a subject taught in local schools and there must be at least 100 shrimp boats which tie up in local ports. Each year one of the many festivals is the blessing of the shrimp fleet ...and you can buy the most beautiful pink shrimp in local seafood stores.

During the winter of 1983, I had the pleasure (both mentally and gastronomically) of writing "The Shrimp Lover's Cookbook". When the publisher finally assembled the book, there was insufficient room for several of the recipes I had submitted.

Therefore, without any duplication, I've been able to include several of my favorites which could not be included in that book.

Who says a recipe has to be complicated to be good? Here's one with only three ingredients and guaranteed to bring forth compliments!

Bacon Wrap-arounds

INGREDIENTS (makes 12)

6	Slices	Bacon
3	Tsps.	Prepared mustard
12		Raw shrimp, shelled and deveined, with tip of tail shell left intact

DIRECTIONS

- Partially cook bacon. Spread each bacon slice with about 1/2 teaspoon of mustard.

- Cut each piece of bacon in half. Wrap around shrimp and secure with a toothpick.

- Broil, about 4 inches from flame, until bacon is crisp, about 2 to 3 minutes on each side.

Marinated Shrimp

INGREDIENTS (serves up to 24, as an appetizer)

3	Pounds	Raw shrimp, cooked, shelled and deveined
2		Lemons, unpeeled, sliced paper thin
1	Large	Onion, sliced paper thin
1 1/3	Cups	Olive oil
2/3	Cups	Tarragon vinegar
		Juice of 2 lemons
2	Tsp.	Salt
1/2	Tsp.	Black pepper, freshly ground

DIRECTIONS

- Place the cooked shrimp in a bowl with the sliced lemons and onion. Place all other ingredients in a jar with a tight-fitting cover. Shake vigorously and pour over shrimp.

- Cover and refrigerate overnight. Serve the shrimp in their marinade with toothpicks for spearing.

Shrimp Delight

INGREDIENTS (serves 4)

1 1/2	Pounds	Medium raw shrimp
4	Tbsps.	Butter
1	Tsp.	Worcestershire sauce
1	Clove	Garlic, minced
2	Tbsps.	Chives, chopped
2	Tbsps.	Parsley flakes
1/4	Tsp.	Salt
1/8	Tsp.	Black pepper, freshly ground
1/4	Cup	Grated parmesan cheese
1/4	Cup	Dry bread crumbs

DIRECTIONS

- Shell and devein the shrimp. Pat them dry with paper towels.

- Melt the butter in a medium skillet. Add the shrimp, Worcestershire sauce, garlic, chives, parsley flakes, salt and pepper. Saute for about 5 minutes, stirring constantly, until shrimp just turn pink.

- With a slotted spoon, transfer the shrimp to a casserole dish. Sprinkle them with the cheese and bread crumbs. Pour the butter in which the shrimp were cooked over all.

- Bake, in a preheated 400° oven, for 8 to 10 minutes, until golden brown. Serve with drawn butter, garnished with a sprig of parsley and a lemon wedge.

Shrimp-Crab Chowder

INGREDIENTS (serves 4)

1/2	Cup	Butter
1	Medium	Onion, finely diced
1/4	Cup	Flour
2	Tsp.	Salt
1/2	Tsp.	White Pepper
1/4	Tsp.	Mace
4	Cups	Light cream
1/2	Pound	Small raw shrimp, shelled and deveined
1	Cup	Cooked crab meat
1/4	Cup	Dry sherry

DIRECTIONS

- In a large saucepan, melt the butter over medium heat. Add the onions and saute until they are soft.

- Stir in the flour, salt, pepper and mace. Add the cream, a little at a time, while stirring constantly, until sauce thickens.

- Add the shrimp, lower heat and cook, uncovered, for about 15 minutes, stirring periodically.

- Add the crab meat and cook until crab is heated through.

- Stir in the sherry and serve.

So you don't like a heavy batter on your shrimp.
Then...this recipe is for you.

Egg Fried Shrimp

INGREDIENTS (serves 6)

1 1/2	Pounds	Raw shrimp, shelled and deveined
1/2	Cup	Lemon juice
1	Cup	Flour
3		Eggs, beaten
1 1/2	Tsp.	Salt
1/4	Tsp.	Black pepper, freshly ground

DIRECTIONS

• Cut shrimp down back to last tail section
  and spread out butterfly style.

• Pour lemon juice over shrimp and allow
  to set for 15 minutes.

• Place flour in a paper bag. Add shrimp
  and toss to coat shrimp well with flour.

• Combine eggs, salt and pepper. Dip each
  shrimp into eggs.

• Heat about 1/8 inch of oil in a skillet
  and, when hot, drop in enough shrimp to
  cover bottom.

• Brown shrimp on both sides, frying them
  for about 4 minutes.

• Remove and add more shrimp. Drain on
  paper towels.

*Every once in a while we have some boiled rice left over from a
Cuban or Oriental meal. Usually, a day or two later—fried rice
is on the menu. It's almost never the same, because the ingredients
depend upon what leftovers we have in the refrigerator*.
The following recipe, which utilizes shrimp, is one of my favorites.*

Shrimp Fried Rice

INGREDIENTS (serves 4)

3	Tbsps	Vegetable or peanut oil
2		Eggs, lightly beaten
1		Dried red chili pepper
2	Cloves	Garlic, diced
1	Tbsp.	Fresh ginger, peeled and diced
1	Pound	Raw shrimp, shelled and deveined, cut into 1/4" pieces
1	Medium	Carrot, cut into 1/4" dice
1	Medium	Onion, diced
1/2	Cup	Fresh mushrooms, sliced
1/2	Tsp.	Salt
1/8	Tsp.	Black pepper, freshly ground
2	Cups	Cold cooked rice
1	Tbsp.	Soy sauce
2		Scallions, cut into 1/4" rings

DIRECTIONS

- In a wok or large skillet, heat 1 teaspoon of the oil over
  medium heat. Tip the wok in all directions to coat it evenly.

- Pour in the beaten eggs and cook, undisturbed, until
  the eggs are half-set, about 1/2 minute. Before the
  eggs are completely set, transfer to a dish. Cut up
  the eggs into 1/4" strips. Set aside.

- Clean the wok, wipe dry and return to the stove.
  Add 1 tablespoon of oil and, over high heat, tip wok to coat
  sides.

- When hot, add the red pepper. Cook for about 1/2
  minute, then remove and discard the pepper. Add
  the garlic and ginger. Stir fry about for 2 seconds

SHRIMP FRIED RICE (continued)

(no longer), then add the shrimp and stir fry for about 2 minutes, until cooked through and nicely browned. Transfer the shrimp to the dish with the eggs.

- Return wok to the stove and add 2 teaspoons of oil. Tip wok to coat with oil. When hot, add the carrots, onions and mushrooms. Sprinkle with salt and pepper. Stir fry until onions begin to wilt, about 1 minute. Transfer to dish with eggs and shrimp.

- Return wok to the stove, add 1 tablespoon oil, heat over medium heat. Tip wok to coat with oil.

- Add the rice and stir fry for about 5 minutes, until rice is nicely coated with oil and has become somewhat golden brown.

- Stir in the reserved egg, shrimp and vegetables. Stir until thoroughly mixed and hot. Add the soy sauce. Taste and adjust seasonings.

- Transfer to a serving dish and sprinkle with scallions. Serve.

NOTES

- Fried rice may be kept in a warm oven in a covered casserole for as long as a half hour without drying out. It can also be made several days ahead and frozen. Just leave at room temperature for 2 hours before rewarming in the oven.

* You can really have some fun with this dish. In addition to shrimp (or instead of) feel free to clean out the refrigerator. Use...bacon, ham, spam, pork, chicken, lobster...veggies such as... celery, broccoli, peas, cauliflower. YOU NAME IT...YOU'll LIKE IT.

There's something extra special about a dish that arrives at the table flaming. I think you'll enjoy this one. Remember to turn the lights down just as you bring it out...to create that perfect atmosphere.

Shrimp Under Fire

INGREDIENTS (serves 6)

2	Pounds	Large raw shrimp
1/2	Cup	Dark rum (80 proof)
1/2	Stick	Butter
1/4	Cup	Parsley, minced
1	Tbsp.	Lemon juice
2	Cloves	Garlic, crushed
1	Tsp.	Salt
1/8	Tsp.	Black pepper, freshly ground
2	Tbsps.	Dark rum (80 proof)

DIRECTIONS

* Leaving tails on, peel and devein the shrimp. Rinse the shrimp. Cutting not quite through, split them lengthwise. Flatten them slightly.

* Combine all remaining ingredients (except 2 tablespoons rum) in a shallow frying pan. Heat. Add shrimp, turning to coat well. Cook over low heat until shrimp turn pink and tender.

* Splash 2 tablespoons rum over shrimp. Ignite shrimp immediately and serve.

Fishing in the Keys

The Florida Keys are world renowned as a fisherman's paradise. From large game fish, down to fish just the size of your frying pan, the waters in the Keys yield a delightful harvest …and great sport in the process.

Almost every afternoon, as I sit on my deck, I hear the sound of hand-held electric meat slicers at work filleting the day's catch. Pelicans await just a few feet away…noisily proclaiming that all but those fillets are theirs!

It is said that when times are hard, Key West natives can get along by eating "Grits and Grunts." Grunts are a frequently caught fish, about 6 to 10 inches long, which make a grunting sound when caught. Grunt fillets make good eating...even in the good times.

Grits, Grunts and Johnny Cake

Cook white grits:
One cup of grits with a little salt in four cups of water.

Cook Grunts (which are called pork chops) or grouper, with a couple of onions, salt and pepper and water to barely cover. Place about 3 cut up potatoes or sweet potatoes, as desired, in broth with fish. Add either Key lime juice, lemon or "Old Sour" (salted Key lime juice...mostly used by Conch's with their boiled fish.)

Last but not least, you'll want a Johnny Cake, served hot with butter. Combine: 2 cups of self-rising flour, a speck of salt, 2 tablespoons cooking oil or Crisco, and 2/3 cups of either milk or water. Blend or mix all together and place into a medium size greased iron skillet. Place over low fire and check after 10 minutes. Turn onto other side to finish cooking.

One may prepare all three dishes on different burners, so they will be hot when served.

Mrs. Allen E. Curry
Honorable Mention
Key West Citizen
Cooking Contest

I'm a member of the FMCA (Family Motor Coach Association). In order to belong, a member must own "a self-propelled completely self-contained vehicle which contains all the conveniences of a home, including cooking, sleeping and sanitary facilities, and in which the driver's seat is accessible in a walking position from the living quarters." WHEW!!

Each year the FMCA has a national rally. In 1984 it was held in Ft. Myers, Florida, and more than 2500 motor coach owners attended, myself included. While there, we attended a seminar on "Florida Seafood Cookery" presented by Marilyn Rose, State Seafood Home economist, representing Florida's Department of Natural Resources. She says that the following is her "most favorite in the world" way of eating fish.

Smoked Fish Pate

INGREDIENTS (makes about 3 1/2 cups of spread)

3	Cups	Smoked fish
2	Packages	Cream cheese (8 ounces each), softened
3	Tbsps.	Lemon juice
2	Tbsps.	Onion, grated
3	Tbsps.	Parsley, chopped
		Parsley sprigs (for garnish)
		Assorted crackers

DIRECTIONS

- Remove skin and bones from fish and then separate into individual flakes with a fork.

- Combine the cream cheese, lemon juice and grated onion. Whip until smooth and fluffy.

- Stir in the flaked fish and the parsley. Chill for one hour.

- Garnish with sprigs of parsley. Serve with assorted crackers.

It was Rusty Garland's turn to cook. She prepared a delicious seafood casserole. Rusty had obtained the recipe from Vera Green, whose husband is an executive of "Gorton's of Glouchester", one of this country's largest seafood packers. This recipe will give a clue as to why Gorton's products are so popular.

Haddock and Shrimp Casserole

INGREDIENTS (serves 8)

4	Pounds	Haddock fillets (or any other "white" fish.) In the Keys use grouper, snapper or grunt
1	Pound	Small fresh shrimp, boiled, shelled, deveined and cut in half
2	Cans	Cream of mushroom soup
1	Tsp.	Worcestershire sauce
2	Sticks	Butter (4 ounces each)
2	Stacks	Ritz crackers (from a 12 ounce package of 3 stack packs)

DIRECTIONS

• Heat one quart of water in a 4 quart saucepan until it boils. Add the fish, allow water to return to a boil and simmer fish just until it separates when tested with a fork, about 5 minutes. With a slotted spoon, transfer the fish to a large casserole dish. Discard water in which fish was cooked.

• Arrange the shrimp in a layer on top of the fish.

• Combine the mushroom soup and the Worcestershire sauce. Pour over the shrimp.

• Melt the butter in a medium skillet. Crumble the crackers and add to the butter. Over medium heat, while stirring frequently, slightly brown the cracker crumbs. Sprinkle the crumb mixture over the soup in the casserole.

74

HADDOCK AND SHRIMP CASSEROLE (continued)

- Bake, in a preheated 325° oven, for 40 minutes.
  Serve hot.

HINT

- Do not use any salt in any part of this recipe. The
  soup, butter and crackers contain sufficient salt for
  the final product.

- If fresh shrimp are unavailable, use 2 cans (7 ounces
  each) which have been drained and "refreshed" in
  cold water for 15 minutes.

Fillets Duglere

INGREDIENTS (serves 4)

1 1/2	Pounds	Red snapper, yellowtail, grouper, or other white-fleshed fish fillets
1	Tsp.	Vegetable oil
1/4	Tsp.	Salt
1/8	Tsp.	Black pepper, freshly ground
4	Medium	Tomatoes, peeled, seeded and chopped
1/2	Cup	Dry white wine
4	Tbsps.	Butter
4	Tbsps.	Flour
2	Cups	Milk (or fish broth, or a combination)
1/2	Tsp.	Salt
1		Clove

FILLETS DUGLERE (continued)

DIRECTIONS

- Cut fillets into pieces about 2 inches square. Oil a baking dish and arrange fillets in a single layer. Sprinkle lightly with salt and pepper. Scatter the chopped tomatoes on top and pour in the wine. Cover tightly with foil.

- Bake, in a preheated 375° oven, just until flesh turns from translucent to opaque. To test for doneness, pierce fish at its thickest point with a fork. Twist the fork…when done, the surface should flake. This can take from 15 to 30 minutes, depending upon thickness of fillets. Do not overcook.

- While the fish bake, melt the butter in a saucepan over moderate heat. Stir in the flour. Gradually add the milk (or fish broth), a little at a time, while stirring constantly, until a smooth sauce forms. Add salt and the clove and simmer gently until fish finishes baking.

- When cooked, carefully remove fillets with a spatula, drain well and place on a serving plate. Keep fish warm in the turned off oven, with door ajar, until sauce is finished.

- Place the baking dish over heat on the top of the stove and reduce liquid by half.

- Remove the clove from sauce and combine with reduced cooking liquid. Spoon this sauce over fish.

Baked Dolphin

INGREDIENTS (serves 4)

4		Dolphin fillets
		Salt
		Juice of one lime
3	Medium	Onions, sliced
1	Small	Eggplant, peeled and cubed
3	Medium	Tomatoes, chopped
6	Blades	Chives, chopped (1 Tbsp.)
1 1/2	Tbsps.	Butter
3	Tbsps.	Flour
2	Cups	Milk
1	Dash	Angostura bitters
1	Tsp.	Salt
1/2	Tsp.	Black pepper, freshly ground

DIRECTIONS

• Skin and rinse the fillets. Pat dry with paper towels.
  Sprinkle with salt and rub well with lime juice.

• Arrange fillets in a buttered baking dish and cover
  with the onions, eggplant, tomatoes and chives.

• Melt the butter in a small saucepan. Stir in the
  flour. Gradually add the milk, a little at a time,
  until a smooth sauce has formed.

• Add the Angostura bitters, salt and pepper. Pour
  this sauce over the fish fillets.

• Bake, uncovered, in a preheated 350° oven, for about
  50 minutes until the fish is cooked and lightly
  browned on top.

Nanci R. LaRe
Key West Citizen
Cooking Contest

Sweet and Spicy Mutton Snapper

INGREDIENTS (serves 6 to 8)

3	Pounds	Mutton snapper fillets
1	Cup	Flour
1	Tsp.	Salt
1/4	Tsp.	Black pepper, freshly ground
1	Bottle	Peanut Oil (8 ounces)
2	Medium	Onions, sliced thin
1	Clove	Garlic, chopped
1	Can	Button mushrooms (4 ounces)
1	Can	Crushed pineapple (8 ounces)
1	Tbsp	Kitchen bouquet
2	Tbsps.	Pickapepper sauce

DIRECTIONS

- Wash fillets and pat dry with paper towels. Combine flour, salt and pepper. Dredge fillets in this mixture.

- Heat oil in a large skillet. Add fillets and fry until golden brown. Remove fillets, drain and cool.

- Allow drippings to settle in skillet. Remove enough oil to allow 3 tablespoons of oil plus drippings to remain in pan.

- Saute onion, garlic and mushrooms until onion is transparent.

- Add fillets, pineapple, kitchen bouquet and Pickapepper sauce. Cover with water.

- Simmer gently over low heat for 45 minutes. More salt and pepper may be added to taste.

- Serve over hot fluffy rice.

Captain Bucky Hoffman
Key West Citizen
Cooking Contest

At Mile Marker 15 there is an unassuming little bar and restaurant call Bay Point Inn. When visiting Key West, take the short trip out to this restaurant...it may just have the best food in or near Key West.

Seafood Divan
...ala Bay Point Inn

INGREDIENTS (serves 4)

3	Tbsps.	Butter
4	Tbsps.	Flour
1 1/2	Cups	Chicken stock (fresh or canned)
1/4 - 1/2	Cup	Heavy cream
1/4	Cup	Swiss cheese, grated
		Salt
		White pepper
1	Pound	Flowerets of fresh broccoli
2	Pounds	Fresh seafood, cleaned (fish, scallops, shrimp, crab)
4	Tbsps.	Butter
4	Ounces	Dry sherry
4	Tbsps.	Parmesan cheese

DIRECTIONS

• First we'll make a Mornay sauce. Melt the butter in a small stainless steel saucepan. Add the flour and stir. Add the chicken stock, a little at a time and while stirring constantly, until a smooth sauce forms. Stir in 1/4 cup of the heavy cream. If the sauce seems too thick (it should flow fairly easily off the spoon), add as much of the remaining cream as necessary. Stir in the Swiss cheese and season to taste with salt and white pepper. Set the Mornay sauce aside.

• Place the broccoli in a steamer over a bath of boiling water and steam until crisp.

SEAFOOD DIVAN (continued)

- While broccoli steams, saute the seafood in butter.
  When just cooked, drain and return to heat...
  add the sherry, toss once and drain again.

- Arrange broccoli along one side of individual
  serving dishes, with flowerets outermost. Divide
  seafood over broccoli stems. Cover seafood with
  Mornay sauce, sprinkle with Parmesan cheese and
  brown under broiler. Serve hot.

Dolphin Baked in Strawberry Honey

INGREDIENTS (serves 4)

1	Cup	Honey (clover or another with mild flavor)
1/2	Cup	Chablis (or other white wine)
		Juice of 1 small lemon
1/4	Cup	Brandy (optional)
1	Pint	Strawberries, washed, stemmed and sliced
4	Fillets	Dolphin (about 2 pounds)

DIRECTIONS

- Combine honey, wine, lemon juice and brandy. Add
  strawberries.

- In a shallow baking dish, pour a little of the honey
  and wine mixture. Add fillets and pour remaining
  liquid over, coating all the fish. Arrange strawberry
  slices on top.

- Bake, in a preheated 400° oven, for about 15
  minutes, until fish turns white and will flake, and
  the liquid bubbles.

Annie Weimer Levin
Key West Citizen
Cooking Contest

Island Favorites

Key West is the Southernmost city in the United States...
and because of this climate...many tropical fruits abound.

This section presents a few popular local recipes utilizing
some of these fruits.

Also, see the section entitled "S'more Desserts"...most of
these recipes also utilize locally grown fruits.

To make this Filipino dish, you'll need green papaya, lemon grass and your own pepper bush...from which you'll use the leaves.

Chicken Soup with Green Papaya

INGREDIENTS (serves 4)

1		Fresh chicken, skin and fat removed, cut into 1 inch pieces (about 3 pounds)
3	Medium	Onions, sliced
2	Medium	Tomatoes, seeds removed, cut into pieces
10	Pieces	Lemon grass, folded and tied to facilitate removal when cooking has completed
1	Piece	Fresh ginger, 2 inches long, smashed with the handle of a knife, so flavor can be extracted, yet ginger can be re-moved in one piece after cooking
1		Green papaya (which is full size but not yet turned yellow) peeled and seeded, cut into 8 large wedges, then cut into 1/2 inch slices
6		Scallions, both white and green part, cut into 1/4 inch rings
		Salt
		Black pepper, freshly ground
8	Ounces	Fresh bright large leaves from any pepper plant (spinach may be used)...optional

DIRECTIONS

- Place chicken, onion, tomato, lemon grass and ginger in a large pot. Barely cover with water and simmer gently, covered, until chicken is cooked, about 40 minutes.

- Add papaya, replace cover, and continue cooking until papaya is soft, about 20 minutes.

- Season to taste with salt and pepper. Turn off heat and add pepper leaves and scallions on top. Don't stir. Cover until ready to serve.

This tart fruit makes excellent marmalade.

Calamondin Marmalade

INGREDIENTS (makes 5 half pints)

1	Quart	Slivered calamondin rind and chopped fruit (about 1 3/4 pounds of ripe calamondins)
2	Cups	Water
8-10	Cups	Sugar

DIRECTIONS

• Cut the fruit in half lengthwise, then scrape out and discard the seeds and pith. Cut rind into fine slivers about 1/2 inch long, saving fruit and juice.

• Mix the rind, fruit and juice in a large stainless steel saucepan. Add the water and simmer, uncovered, for 10 minutes. Cover and refrigerate overnight.

• Next day, wash and sterilize 5 half pint jars and closures. Stand them on a baking sheet and keep hot in a 250° oven until needed.

• Measure the fruit mixture and for each cup add 2 to 2 1/2 cups of sugar.

• Return fruit and sugar to the pan, insert a candy thermometer and slowly heat uncovered to boiling, stirring until sugar dissolves. Boil slowly, uncovered while stirring periodically, until thermometer reaches 218-220°.

• Gather a little of the juice in a large metal spoon, cool slightly, then tilt. If the drops slide together in a sheet, the marmalade is done.

• Remove from heat, stir for 1 minute, then skim off froth and ladle into jars, filling to within 1/8" of top.

• Wipe rims and seal. Cool, check seals, label and store in a cool, dry place.

Mango chutney is a tart, gingery relish used to accompany hot or cold meats, chicken and seafoods. Perhaps the most famous available commercially is Major Grey's chutney.

Mango Chutney...No. 1

INGREDIENTS (makes 3 pints)

2	Ounces	Dried tamarind (a piece of the pod about 2 inches long, see Note)
1/2	Cup	Boiling water
4	Pounds	Medium-sized unripe mangos
2	Cups	Malt vinegar
1	Cup	Sugar
1	Medium	Onion, finely chopped
1/2	Cup	Seedless raisins
1/2	Cup	Ginger root, peeled and finely chopped
2	Cloves	Garlic, finely diced
1	Tsp.	Fresh hot chili, stem and seeds removed, finely diced (See Note)
1/2	Tsp.	Ground allspice
2	Tbsps.	Salt

DIRECTIONS

- Place the tamarind in a small bowl and pour the boiling water over it. Let the tamarind soak for one hour, stirring and mashing occasionally with a spoon, until the pulp softens and breaks up in the water. Place a fine sieve over a bowl, and pour the soaking liquid through it. Rub the tamarind through the sieve, pressing down hard with the back of a spoon before discarding the seeds and fibers.

- Peel the mangos and cut the flesh away from the large flat seed. Discard the seed and cut the mangos into 1 inch pieces.

MANGO CHUTNEY (continued)

- Combine the mangos and vinegar in a 4 quart stain-less steel pot. Bring to a boil over high heat and cook briskly for 10 minutes, stirring occasionally. Stir in the sugar, onion, raisins, ginger root, garlic, chili, allspice and salt. Reduce the heat to low and simmer uncovered for 45 minutes, or until mango flesh is tender, stirring periodically. Stir more frequently toward end to prevent scorching.

- Wash and sterilize 3 (1 pint) jars and their closures, and stand them on a baking sheet in a 250° oven until needed.

- Remove pot from heat and ladle the chutney immedi-ately into hot sterilized canning jars, filling them to within 1/8 inch of the top. Seal each jar quickly and tightly with sterilized rings and lids.

NOTES

- Tamarind trees grow in the Keys. The seed pod is brittle, cinnamon-colored and shaped somewhat like a pea pod, but is up to 8 inches long. The soft acid tasting pulp of the pod is used as a flavoring in preserves and in chutneys.

- Hot chilies can burn your skin when you handle them. Wear rubber gloves (or a "Baggie") when you handle them.

Here's a simplified recipe for mango Chutney you may enjoy trying.

Mango Chutney...No. 2

INGREDIENTS

1	Cup	Water
5	Tbsps.	Sugar
3	Tbsps.	Vinegar
1/2	Tsp.	Allspice
1/4	Tsp.	Salt
1	Tsp.	Dry mustard
1	Whole	Ginger root, peeled and diced
1		Apple, peeled, cored and cut into small pieces
6		Mangos, peeled and seeded, cut into small pieces
1		Green pepper, stem and seeds removed, cut into small pieces (pepper may be hot or sweet, as you prefer)
1/2	Cup	Seedless raisins

DIRECTIONS

• In a large saucepan, combine the water, sugar, vinegar, allspice, salt, mustard, and ginger root. Cook for 5 minutes.

• Add apples, mango, pepper and raisins. Simmer for 45 minutes. Chill.

SERVING SUGGESTIONS

• Serve as a condiment for curry.

• On a platter place cream cheese surrounded by Triscuit crackers. Top generously with Mango Chutney.

Jeanette C. Downey
Key West Citizen
Cooking Contest

Old Sour is a condiment used to flavor meats and seafood. It is available in 16 ounce bottles labeled "Nellie and Joe's Old Sour". If you have access to Key limes you may follow this recipe and make your own.

Old Sour

INGREDIENTS (makes 1 pint)

2	Cups	Key Lime juice
1	Tbsp.	Salt
		Hot bird peppers *

DIRECTIONS

• Combine the Key lime juice and salt. Mix thoroughly.

• Strain the liquid through cheesecloth 4 times.

• Pour the liquid into a bottle, add the peppers and allow it to age in the refrigerator for about 2 weeks.

NOTES:

• Sprinkle Old Sour on fish, or add to Corn-and-Bean Soup. We also use it as a dip for roast pork.

• Old Sour will be good for 2 to 3 months.

* The peppers are not in the commercially produced "Old Sour", but are added by you, the Chef. If you don't have hot bird peppers, use a Jalapeno pepper.

Pickled Green Mango

INGREDIENTS (makes 1 gallon)

6-8		Green mangos
4	Tbsps.	Coarse salt
2	Cloves	Garlic, crushed
3	1/4" slices	Fresh ginger root, peeled
1	Gallon	Wide mouth jar, sterilized
		Water

DIRECTIONS

• Select mangos that are full size, hard and still green. Leave the skin on. Scrub them. Cut them into lengthwise strips (about the same size as Kosher dill pickles).

• Place mango slices, salt, garlic and ginger into a sterilized gallon jar. Fill balance of jar with water. Be certain that mangos are completely covered with water.

• Set jar on counter for 2 to 3 weeks, shaking occasionally. After this period, store pickles in a cool, dry place.

Compliments of:
May DelaCruz
Key West

Mango and Avocado Salad

INGREDIENTS (serves 4)

2	Heads	Boston or bibb lettuce, washed and patted dry
2	Medium	Sweet red peppers, stem and seeds removed, cut into thin rings
1	Medium	Red Spanish onion (or white Vidalia, in season), cut into thin rings, separated
1	Large	Sweet mango (or 2 medium), ripe but firm, (should be relatively free from fiber), peeled and cut into wedges lengthwise
1	Large	Avocado (or 2 medium), ripe but firm, peeled and cut into wedges lengthwise
2	Tbsps.	Lemon juice
1/2	Cup	Olive oil
4-6	Tbsps.	Red wine vinegar (or Balsamic)
1/2	Tsp.	Tamari soy sauce
1	Tsp.	Dried sweet marjoram leaves
1	Pinch	Sugar
		Black pepper, freshly ground

DIRECTIONS

• Arrange lettuce leaves on salad plates or in salad bowls.

• Combine pepper and onion slices in a bowl and toss until mixed.

• Carefully, so as not to break wedges, place the mango and avocado slices in a bowl and sprinkle with lemon juice.

• In a blender, mix the oil, vinegar, soy sauce, marjoram and sugar until emulsified.

- Arrange onion-pepper rings atop lettuce leaves.

- Arrange mango and avocado wedges alternately atop rings, taking care not to break them.

- Dribble dressing over all, sprinkle with pepper to taste and serve immediately.

Rand B. Lee
Winner
Key West Citizen
Cooking Contest

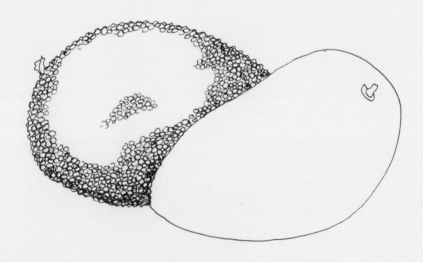

Green Papaya Salad

INGREDIENTS (serves 4)

2	Cups	Green papaya, peeled, seeds removed, washed and diced
1/4	Tsp.	Salt
1	Tsp.	Lime juice
1/2	Tsp.	Mustard
1	Tsp.	Chopped parsley
1/4	Tsp.	Salt
1/8	Tsp.	Black pepper, freshly ground
3		Hard cooked eggs, chopped
2	Whole	Red pimientos, chopped
1 1/2	Tbsps.	Mayonnaise
4		Crisp lettuce leaves

DIRECTIONS

- Place papaya and salt in a small saucepan. Cover with water and simmer for about 20 minutes, until tender. Drain and chill.

- Add lime juice, mustard, parsley, salt, pepper, eggs, pimiento and mayonnaise. Blend ingredients and chill for 1 hour.

- Serve on crisp lettuce leaves. Sprinkle each with parsley before serving.

Mrs. Bertha Curry
Key West Citizen
Cooking Contest

One of the fruit trees which grow in Key West is called a "Sapodilla".
It has a brown fruit, about 3 inches in diameter, which is delicious.
To many Filipinos who reside in Key West, the tree and fruit are
called "Chico", and it is the source of chiclet, with which we are familiar
in chewing gum.

Sapodilla Nut Bread

INGREDIENTS (makes 1 loaf)

1	Stick	Butter, softened
1	Cup	Brown sugar
1/2	Cup	Vegetable oil
4		Eggs, beaten
3	Cups	Flour
2	Tsps.	Baking soda
2 1/2	Tsps.	Cinnamon
1 1/2	Tsps.	Allspice
1	Cup	Sapodillas, mashed
1	Cup	Walnuts or pecans, chopped
1	Cup	Raisins

DIRECTIONS

- Cream the butter and sugar together. Blend in the oil. Add the eggs and beat well.

- Sift together the flour, baking soda, cinnamon and allspice.

- Add dry ingredients, alternately with the mashed sapodilla. Add the nuts and raisins and pour into a greased loaf pan.

- Bake, in a preheated 350° oven, for one hour or until a fork inserted into center of loaf comes out clean. Serve hot for breakfast.

Cynthia Rohe
Third Prize
Key West Citizen
Cooking Contest

Key Lime Pies

When you visit the Keys, you'll find signs, menus, and post cards...bakeries and restaurants...all proclaiming that they have or serve..."authentic" Key Lime Pie. Each will naturally proclaim theirs to be the best.

Rather than accept as gospel any authority in this friendly controversy...decide for yourself...by sampling a variety of Key Lime Pies while you are here. Regardless of which you ultimately consider the best...you'll have fun testing each and deciding.

And just so you can reminisce and relive your visit, here is a whole chapter full of Key Lime Pie recipes.

My mother, who lives in Massachusetts, sent me an article
which appeared in the Boston Globe, *written by Bob Morse of*
the Orlando Sentinel, *about authentic Key Lime Pie as made in*
Key West…so that I, living in Key West, could tell you how to make it.
Now, if that isn't the long way around the barn…!

"Authentic" Key Lime Pie

INGREDIENTS (serves 8)

1		Pie shell, unbaked
3	Jumbo	Eggs (or 4 large eggs)
1/2	Cup	Key lime juice
1	Can	Eagle brand sweetened condensed milk (14 ounces)
1/2	Tsp.	Cream of tartar
1/8	Tsp.	Salt
4	Tbsps.	Sugar
1/2	Tsp.	Vanilla

DIRECTIONS

- Prebake the pie shell as directions indicate.

- Separate the eggs. Beat the yolks in a bowl until thick. Add the condensed milk to the yolks and beat again. Add the Key lime juice and beat until thick.

- Beat the egg whites until frothy, using a rotary beater or electric mixer at moderate speed. Add cream of tartar and salt. Continue beating, while adding sugar, one tablespoon at a time.

- When all sugar has been incorporated, add vanilla and beat hard (highest mixer speed) until glossy and peaks stand straight up when beaters are withdrawn.

- Add about 1/4 of the egg white mixture to the filling. Pour the filling into the pie crust.

AUTHENTIC KEY LIME PIE (continued)

- Top the filling with the remaining meringue, taking care to seal the meringue to the pie crust all around.

- Bake, in a preheated 350° oven, for about 15 minutes, or until meringue is golden brown.

- Allow to cool for about 2 hours before refrigerating.

HINTS:

- To obtain a firm pie filling, use only Eagle Brand Sweetened Condensed Milk.

- Key lime pie is yellow, not green.

- Authentic Key Lime Pie is made with a pastry crust...not a graham-cracker crust.

Flaky Pastry

INGREDIENTS (makes one crust for 9 inch pie)

1 1/4	Cups	Flour, sifted
1/2	Tsp.	Salt
1/3	Cup	Vegetable shortening or lard, chilled
1/4	Cup	Ice water

DIRECTIONS

- Place flour and salt in a shallow mixing bowl. Cut in the shortening with a pastry blender until mixture resembles coarse meal.

- Sprinkle water over surface, a tablespoon at a time. Mix in lightly, with a fork, just until pastry holds together.

- Shape gently into a ball, on a lightly floured surface, then flatten into a circle, about one inch thick, evening up rough edges.

- Sprinkle lightly with flour. With a rolling pin, roll out with short, firm strokes, into a circle about 3 inches larger than your pan.

- To transfer pastry to pan, lay rolling pin across center of pastry circle, fold half of pastry over pin, and ease into pan. Press slightly.

- Seal any cracks or holes by pressing dampened scraps of pastry on top. Trim pastry so it hangs evenly one inch over rim. Roll overhang under, even with rim and crimp or flute as desired.

To Bake Unfilled Pie Crust

- Prick bottom and sides of pastry well with a fork.

- Lay a large square of wax paper over crust and fill with uncooked rice or dried beans. (These may be saved in a jar and used over and over for this purpose.)

- Bake pastry, in a preheated 425° oven, for 10 to 12 minutes, just until tan.

- Lift out paper of rice. Cool before filling.

However, if you prefer the graham cracker crust...here's the recipe.

Graham Cracker Crust

INGREDIENTS (makes 1 crust)

1 1/4	Cups	Graham cracker crumbs
1/4	Cup	Sugar
1/4	Cup	Butter (no more)

DIRECTIONS

- Mix crumbs and sugar together. Melt butter and mix it into crumbs. Press into a pie plate.

- Bake, in a preheated 325° oven, for 8 minutes.

If you start asking around Key West for the authentic recipe for Key Lime Pie, you'll eventually discover that there are at least several, each with supporters claiming that theirs is the recipe. This one comes from an old souvenir brochure, loaned to me by my next door neighbor, Diane Duane.

Key Lime Pie

INGREDIENTS (serves 8)

4		Eggs
1	Can	Eagle Brand sweetened condensed milk
1/3	Cup	Key lime juice
1		Baked pie shell

DIRECTIONS

- Beat the yolks of 4 eggs and the white of 1 until thick. Add the condensed milk and beat again. Add the lime juice and beat until thick.

- Rinse off the beaters. Using a clean bowl, beat the 3 remaining egg whites until dry and fold into the mixture.

- Pour into the baked pie shell and bake, in a pre-heated 300° oven, until set, about 15 to 20 minutes.

- Allow to cool and then refrigerate until time to serve.

Islander Lime Pie

INGREDIENTS (serves 6 - 8)

1		Pastry crust
1 1/4	Cups	Granulated sugar
1	Envelope	Unflavored gelatin
3		Egg yolks
3/4	Cup	Evaporated milk
3/4	Cup	Fresh lime juice, strained
4	Tbsps.	Grated lime rind
3		Egg whites
1	Cup	Heavy cream
2	Tbsps.	Confectioners sugar

DIRECTIONS

- Bake pastry crust as directed for Key Lime Pie.

- In a heavy 1 quart saucepan, mix the granulated sugar and gelatin. Beat the egg yolks into the sugar mixture. Slowly stir in the evaporated milk. Place the mixture on medium heat and cook, stirring constantly, until it coats a spoon. Do not allow mixture to boil.

- Pour the mixture into a large bowl. Beat in the lime juice and 3 tablespoons of the rind. Allow the mixture to cool to room temperature.

- When the filling has cooled, beat the egg whites until they are very firm.

- With a rubber spatula, stir 1/4 of the egg whites into the filling. Then pour the filling over the remaining egg whites and gently fold together.

- Pour the filling into the prepared pastry shell and refrigerate for at least 2 hours.

- Just before serving, whip the heavy cream until firm enough to stand in soft peaks. Beat in the confectioners sugar and spread cream over the top of the pie.

- Sprinkle top with the remaining tablespoon of lime rind.

When a nice neighbor, Carol Smith, heard that I was researching
Key Lime Pies, she gave me the following recipe for homemade
sweetened condensed milk.

Sweetened Condensed Milk

INGREDIENTS (equals 1 can, 14 ounces)

1/3	Cup	Water, boiling
3	Tbsps.	Butter, melted
3/4	Cup	Granulated sugar
1	Cup	Dry milk crystals

DIRECTIONS

Combine boiling water and melted butter in a
blender container. Turn on low speed and then
gradually add the sugar and dry milk. Blend until
smooth.

Store in covered container in refrigerator.

Each year, early in March, we enjoy attending the Marathon Seafood
Festival. It's held at the airport, located at Mile Marker 51.

Featured throughout the day is a seafood dinner…consisting of
stone crab claws, Florida Lobster, shrimp, conch fritters, fried fish,
cole slaw and bread. In the 1980s, the price for all the above was
only $8.00.

A nice lady who was very active in the background, cooking conch
fritters and presiding over her special Key Lime Pie was Vivian
Daniels. She had come up with another delicious, but really simple,
recipe for Key Lime. Pie. Here 'tis.

Key Lime Pie Daniels

1	Can	Magnolia Brand sweetened condensed milk (14 ounces)
1/3	Cup	Lime juice
6	Ounces	Cool Whip
1		Graham cracker pie shell

DIRECTIONS

• In a bowl, mix together the sweetened condensed milk and the lime juice. Fold in the Cool Whip. Mix well and pour into a graham cracker pie shell. Chill until ready to serve.

Vivian Daniels
Marathon, Florida

This recipe offers a pleasant variation to that favorite, Key Lime Pie. I clipped it from a newspaper one day and filed it where I could easily find it. When I decided to use the recipe several weeks later, it took me at least an hour to find it. Then, when I started to prepare the dish…there it was again…written on the side of the cream cheese container! Grrrr!

Key Lime Cheesecake

INGREDIENTS (serves 8)

1	Package	Cream cheese (8 ounces), softened
1	Can	Sweetened condensed milk (14 ounces)
1/3	Cup	Key lime juice (or 1/2 cup regular lime juice)
2	Drops	Green food color (optional)
1		Graham cracker crust

DIRECTIONS

• With an electric mixer, beat together the cream cheese and sweetened condensed milk. Slowly add the Key lime juice and food color. Continue beating until well blended.

• Pour into a prepared graham cracker crust and chill.

There are several dessert recipes in this book which call for just egg yolks. Here's one that uses those leftover whites.

Lime Chiffon Pie

INGREDIENTS (makes 1 pie)

1	Can	Eagle Brand sweetened condensed milk (14 ounces)
1/3	Cup	Lime juice
5	Drops	Yellow food coloring
3		Egg whites (about 1/3 cup)
1/4	Tsp.	Cream of tartar
1		Graham cracker pie crust

DIRECTIONS

• In a medium bowl, combine the sweetened condensed milk, lime juice and yellow food coloring.

• In a small bowl, beat egg whites with cream of tartar until stiff but not dry.

• Gently fold egg whites into sweetened condensed milk mixture. Pour into crust. Chill for 3 hours or until set. Garnish as desired. Chill leftover pie.

S'More Desserts

Tropical fruits grow in abundance here in the Keys. We have papaya, banana, coconut, Key lime, and mango…just to mention a few. As part of the research for this book…I purposely set out to find recipes utilizing these local fruits …so we all could enjoy them.

I've also added Leche Flan, which is an *absolute must* if you're preparing a Cuban meal.

Mango is one of many tropical fruits which grow here in the Keys. When ripe, and the peel is an orange-yellow color, they are delicious eaten out of hand. However, when still green, this fruit makes a most delicious pie.

Green Mango Pie

INGREDIENTS (makes one 9 inch pie)

1 1/4	Cups	Sugar
1	Tsp.	Ground cinnamon
1/2	Tsp.	Ground nutmeg
2	Tbsps.	All purpose flour
3 1/2	Cups	Green mango, peeled and sliced
1	Tbsp.	Lime juice
		Pastry for double crust 9 inch pie

DIRECTIONS

• In a mixing bowl, combine the sugar, cinnamon, nutmeg and flour. Add the mango and lime juice. Stir well and spoon into pastry shell.

• With a pastry brush and water, moisten the pastry around the outside of pie.

• Top with pastry and crimp edges to seal. Cut several slits in the top crust to act as steam vents.

• Bake, in a preheated 450° oven, for 10 minutes. Reduce heat to 375° and continue baking for 40 to 45 minutes, until done.

The only difficult part of this recipe is getting the coconut meat out of the shell...but don't cheat and use commercially processed coconut. There's a world of difference. Instead, have your hubby get out his trusty little hatchet (or possibly that war-souvenir bayonet). Place the coconut on a solid surface and give it a few good whacks to break open the husk. When the husk is off, punch holes in the "eyes" with an ice pick and pour out the water. With the hatchet, again give the shell a hard hit to break it open. Remove the meat with a strong knife, peel off the brown skin and shred the beautiful white meat in your food processor. One coconut makes one pie, so while you're at it, do more than one. The meat freezes well in plastic freezer bags.

Fresh Coconut Pie

INGREDIENTS (makes one pie)

1/4	Cup	Cornstarch
1	Cup	Sugar
1/4	Tsp.	Salt
2	Cups	Milk, scalded
3		Eggs, separated
3/4	Tsp.	Vanilla
2	Tbsps	Butter
1 1/2	Cups	Coconut, shredded
1		Baked pie shell (8 or 9 inches)

DIRECTIONS

• Mix the cornstarch, 2/3 cup of the sugar and the salt in a saucepan. Gradually add the scalded milk, over low heat, stirring constantly. After mixture is thick, continue cooking this custard for two minutes.

• Remove from heat and mix two tablespoons of the custard into the egg yolks. Add the egg mixture to custard and cook, stirring constantly, for two more minutes on low heat.

FRESH COCONUT PIE (continued)

* Turn off heat and stir in the vanilla and butter.
  When butter has melted, fold in 1 cup of the coconut. Let cool.

* Beat egg whites with 1/3 cup of the sugar until stiff
  peaks form.

* Place the custard in pie shell. Top with meringue,
  being careful to seal edges. Sprinkle with remaining
  1/2 cup coconut and bake in a 400° oven until top is
  browned.

* Chill thoroughly before serving.

Toni Murray
Key West

NOTE

* The coconut meat comes out of the shell a little
  easier if, after removing water, you heat the nut in
  a microwave oven for one minute on high heat.

*This dessert is just about perfect. For the cook… it's easy to make.
For the guests …it's light but utterly delicious!*

Rose Mangos

INGREDIENTS (serves 6)

3		Mangos, peeled and sliced
3	Tbsps.	Honey
1/3	Cup	Orange juice
2	Tbsps.	Brandy (or orange liquor)
1/8	Tsp.	Ground cinnamon
1/2	Pint	Heavy cream, whipped
2	Tbsps.	Sugar
1/2	Tsp.	Vanilla extract

DIRECTIONS

- Arrange mango slices in a glass serving dish (one with sides to contain the liquid).

- Heat honey, orange juice and brandy until warm. Pour over mangos and sprinkle with cinnamon.

- Cover and chill until serving time.

- Serve with whipped cream flavored with sugar and vanilla.

Kathy Cloninger, Winner
Key West Citizen Cooking Contest

Mango Mousse

INGREDIENTS (serves 6)

1 1/2	Cups	Mango, peeled and chopped
1/2	Cup	Sugar
2	Tsps.	Fresh lime juice
1	Envelope	Plain gelatin
3/4	Cup	Sour cream
1 1/2	Tsps.	Vanilla

DIRECTIONS

- Combine mango, sugar and lime juice in a bowl. Cover and refrigerate for 30 minutes.

- Pour into a sieve and drain liquid into another bowl. Add gelatin and dissolve well in mango liquid. Combine mango and dissolved gelatin.

- In a clean bowl, beat cream cheese until light. Stir in sour cream and vanilla. Carefully fold mango into cheese mixture.

- Spoon into tall glasses or into a souffle dish. Refrigerate until firm.

NOTE

- This dish freezes well.

Mrs. Florence Fox-Loeb
Key West Citizen Cooking Contest

Calamondins are super tart, tiny citrus fruit available in Florida and California.

Calamondin Cake

INGREDIENTS (makes 1 cake)

- - - - - - For Cake- - - - - -

1	Package	Yellow cake mix (18 1/2 ounces)
	Package	Lemon flavored jello (3 ounces)
1/2	Cup	Calamondin puree (mixture of juice and fruit)
4		Eggs
1/2	Cup	Vegetable oil
1	Tsp.	Lemon flavoring
1/3	Cup	Milk

- - - - - - For Glaze- - - - - -

1 1/2	Cups	Confectioners sugar
4	Tbsps.	Butter, melted
1/2	Cup	Calamondin puree

DIRECTIONS

- In a mixing bowl, combine all cake ingredients and mix well. Pour into a greased and floured 9 X 12 baking pan.

- Bake, in a preheated 350° oven, for 25 minutes or until a toothpick inserted in center comes out clean.

- Combine glaze ingredients and pour over the hot cake.

Vivian Daniels
Marathon, Florida

Just around the corner from Mallory Square, downtown Key West, there was a delightful restaurant...very popular with the locals. Here's one reason why.

Key Lime Cake
(Pigeon House Patio, Key West)

INGREDIENTS (serves 12 to 15)

1 1/3	Cups	Sugar
2	Cups	All purpose flour
2/3	Tsp.	Salt
1	Tsp.	Baking powder
1/2	Tsp.	Baking soda
1	Package	Lime-flavored gelatin (3 ounces)
5		Eggs, lightly beaten
1 1/3	Cups	Cooking oil
3/4	Cup	Orange juice
1/2	Tsp.	Vanilla
1	Tsp.	Lemon extract
1/3	Cup	Key lime juice
1/3	Cup	Powdered sugar
		Whipped cream
		Thin lime slices (or fresh strawberries)

DIRECTIONS

- Place the sugar, flour, salt, baking powder, baking soda and gelatin in a mixing bowl. Add the eggs, oil, orange juice, vanilla and lemon extract. Beat until well blended. Pour the batter into a 9 X 13 inch baking pan.

- Bake, in a preheated 350° oven for 25 to 30 minutes, until a toothpick stuck into the center comes out clean.

- Remove cake from oven. Let stand in the pan for 15 minutes, or until almost cool.

KEY LIME CAKE (Pigeon House Patio, Key West, continued)

- Prick cake all over with a fork. Drizzle thoroughly with lime juice and sprinkle with powdered sugar. Cover and refrigerate.

- To serve, cut into squares, top with whipped cream and garnish with a lime slice (or with a fresh strawberry).

Papaya Delight

INGREDIENTS (makes 2 pies)

1	Can	Magnolia brand sweetened condensed milk
3 to 4	Tbsps.	Lemon juice (or Key lime juice to taste)
1 1/2	Cups	Fully ripened papaya, cut into 1/2 inch chunks
3/4	Cup	Fresh orange sections, cut up and pulp removed (or 1 small can crushed pineapple)
1	Carton	Cool Whip (9 ounces)
1	Cup	Slivered almonds or pecans (save some to sprinkle on top)
2		9 inch pie crusts, baked

DIRECTIONS

- Mix first two ingredients, then add the rest. Fold into baked pie crusts. Chill before serving.

HINTS

- Keeps well in freezer. If frozen, take out in time to reach room temperature.

- Graham cracker crusts may be used.

Mrs. Carolyn Brinkley
Key West Citizen Cooking Contest

To me, no Cuban meal would be complete without Leche Flan.
It's a rich, sweet custard dessert...and a small serving goes a long way.

Leche Flan (Milk Custard)

INGREDIENTS (serves 8)

2	Tbsps.	Light brown sugar
2	Tbsps.	Maple syrup (or coffee syrup)
10		Egg yolks (reserve egg whites for another recipe)
1	Can	Sweetened condensed milk (14 ounces)
1	Can	Evaporated milk (13 ounces)
1	Tsp.	Vanilla (or rum) extract

DIRECTIONS

• Spoon the brown sugar into a 9 inch cake pan (or flan mold). Caramelize sugar by stirring continuously over medium heat until melted. Add syrup and tilt pan to cover the sides of pan.

• In an electric mixer, on low speed, mix together the egg yolks. Then add the condensed milk, evaporated milk and flavoring.

• Set aside for about 5 minutes, to rest, and then skim off any foam on the top.

• Pour, through a strainer, into the caramelized pan. Cover tightly with a double thickness of aluminum foil.

• Place a rack into another pan which is large enough to hold the flan. Add cold water up to height of rack. Place flan on rack.

• Bake, in a preheated 350° oven, for 45-50 minutes, until a toothpick inserted in center comes out clean.

LECHE FLAN (MILK CUSTARD) (continued)

- Allow to cool. Remove foil. Run a knife around the edge of the pan to loosen the flan. Cover the flan with a round serving plate. (It must be larger than the caramelized pan.) While grasping both the serving dish and caramelized pan with both hands, quickly invert. Carefully lift the pan off the flan.

- In the back yard of many houses in the Keys, you'll find banana plants growing. When harvested, here's how some of them end up.

Honey Baked Bananas

INGREDIENTS (serves 4)

4		Firm ripe bananas, peeled and cut in half lengthwise
1	Tbsp.	Butter, melted
1/4	Cup	Honey
1	Tbsp.	Orange juice
1/4	Cup	Pecans, chopped

DIRECTIONS

- Brush bananas with butter and place cut side down in a 13 X 9 X 2 inch dish.

- Combine honey and orange juice. Mix well and pour over bananas. Sprinkle with pecans.

- Bake, in a preheated 375° oven, for 15 minutes.

Key West Drinks

Key West has a permanent population of about 25,000 people. During winter "season" it can swell to around 70,000.

During the summer it's quite hot and the residents are often thirsty. Also, as you might guess, those winter vacationers bring thirst with them. As a result...there are more than a few bars in this city...and over the years several of them have concocted some rather famous drinks.

Here are a few...

Sloppy Joe's Cocktail No. 1

INGREDIENTS (makes 1)

1/4	Tsp.	Triple Sec
1/4	Tsp.	Grenadine
3/4	Ounce	Rum
3/4	Ounce	Dry Vermouth

DIRECTIONS

• Shake with ice and strain into cocktail glass.

Sloppy Joe's Cocktail No. 2

INGREDIENTS (makes 1)

3/4	Ounce	Pineapple juice
3/4	Ounce	5-star brandy
3/4	Ounce	Port
1/4	Ounce	Triple sec
1/4	Tsp.	Grenadine

DIRECTIONS

• Shake with ice and strain into cocktail glass.

Caribbean Sunset

INGREDIENTS (makes 1)

2	Ounces	Tequila Gold
1	Ounce	Lemon juice
1/2	Ounce	Honey
1/4	Tsp.	Grenadine

DIRECTIONS

• Serve in a cocktail glass, with cracked ice.

At the 17 mile marker, there is a fine restaurant known as the Sugarloaf Lodge. Go there…enjoy a meal, and be sure to have one of their world famous strawberry daiquiris!

Strawberry Daiquiri

INGREDIENTS (makes one 14 ounce drink)

2	Ounces	White rum
1	Ounce	Triple Sec
1	Ounce	Sour mix
1	Ounce	Sugar water (simple syrup)
1	Ounce	Orange juice
4	Ounces	Strawberries
4	Ounces	Ice shavings

DIRECTIONS

• Place all ingredients into a blender and blend until thick.

• Pour into large serving glass. Top with whipped cream and a cherry.

SIMPLE SYRUP: Dissolve 1 pound of granulated sugar in 1/2 pint of warm water, gradually adding enough water to make 1 pint of syrup.

Here's a favorite drink from Captain Tony's Saloon...
which was Hemingway's favorite bar from 1933 to 1937.

Captain Tony's "Skullbuster"

INGREDIENTS (makes 1)

2	Shots	"151" Rum (4 ounces)
1	Shot	Meyers Rum (2 ounces)
1	Jigger	Coco Lope cream of coconut (1 1/2 ounces)
1	Ounce	Pineapple juice
1	Ounce	Orange juice
1	Ounce	Grapefruit juice

DIRECTIONS

- Shake well with ice and strain into cocktail glass.
  Do not store in air tight container.

- This delicious fruity wine drink goes perfectly with a Cuban
  meal, or as a punch at parties, or on a hot summer day, or...

Sangria

Ingredients (makes 2 quarts)

1	Quart	Dry red wine
1/2	Cup	Orange juice
1/2	Cup	Sugar
1/4	Cup	Brandy
1	Bottle	Club soda (12 ounces)
		Ice cubes
1		Orange thinly sliced
1		Lemon, thinly sliced

DIRECTIONS

- In a large pitcher or bowl combine the wine, orange
  juice, sugar and brandy. Stir until sugar is dissolved.
  Cover and chill for 2 hours.

- Just before serving, add club soda and ice cubes.
  Garnish with slices of orange and lemon.

DETAILED CONTENTS

THE CUBAN INFLUENCE

CONCH

BLUE CRABS

STONE CRAB

CRAWFISH (FLORIDA LOBSTER)

SHRIMP

FiSHING IN THE KEYS.

ISLAND FAVORITES

KEY LIME PIES

S'MORE DESSERTS

KEY WEST DRINKS

About the Author

William Flagg, a New Englander, comes from a family of cooks. Both his father and grandfather were professional chefs and bakers. His uncle, Andrew Flagg, recently published *The Story of Cape Cod Cooking*.

With this background, it is really no surprise that Mr. Flagg cooked his first meal at age seven. By the time he was seventeen he was a master baker in his father's bakery. After completing a course at the U.S. Navy Cooking School, he served his enlistment as a cook and baker at a naval air station in Florida.

Following military service, Mr. Flagg earned a degree in Industrial Engineering at Northeastern University and a Masters Degree in Business Administration at Bryant College. A career as a Health Systems Engineer has taken him to many cities in the United States and Canada.

A continuing interest in good food and cooking led him to organize and participate in gourmet groups in several cities. He has also taught courses in gourmet cooking to adult education classes.

With this combination of engineering and culinary backgrounds, Mr. Flagg utilizes his experience in technical writing to present each recipe clearly, so that even the inexperienced cook can follow the concise steps with confidence.

When not dining his way around the country in his motor home, gathering recipes, and enjoying local dishes, Mr. Flagg may be found writing and testing recipes in his home in Key West, Florida.

Mr. Flagg is also the author of three other titles, *The Clam Lover's Cookbook*, *The Mushroom Lover's Cookbook*, and *The Shrimp Lover's Cookbook*.